Introductory calculus

The School Mathematics Project

The right of the
University of Cambridge
to print and sell
all manner of books
was granted by
Henry VIII in 1534.
The University has printed
and published continuously
since 1584.

Cambridge University Press

Cambridge   New York   Port Chester   Melbourne   Sydney

Main authors	Stan Dolan
	Andy Hall
	Michael Leach
	Timothy Lewis
	Richard Peacock
	Paul Roder
	Jeff Searle
	David Tall
	Brian Wardle
	Thelma Wilson
	Phil Wood

**Team leader and
project director**   Stan Dolan

The authors would like to give special thanks to Ann White for her help in producing the trial edition and in preparing this book for publication.

Cartoons by Tony Hall

Published by the Press Syndicate of the University of Cambridge
The Pitt Building, Trumpington Street, Cambridge CB2 1RP
40 West 20th Street, New York, NY 10011–4211, USA
10 Stamford Road, Oakleigh, Melbourne 3166, Australia

First published 1991

Printed in Great Britain at the University Press, Cambridge

Cover Design by Iguana Creative Design

Produced by Gecko Limited, Bicester, Oxon.

British Library cataloguing in publication data
16–19 mathematics.
Introductory calculus.
Pupils text.
1. Calculus
I. School Mathematics Project
515

ISBN 0 521 38843 0

Contents

1 Rates of change

Heraclitus

1.1 Introduction

Everything changes! Indeed, the rate at which something changes may be of great significance. Your **speed** is a measure of how your distance changes compared with time, and not paying attention to this 'rate of change' could lead to a public prosecution! Your doctor uses **pulse rate** or heart beats per minute as an indicator of your state of health.

Rates of change do not always involve time; for example, a **conversion rate** (like the monetary exchange rate) enables us to convert from one unit to another.

For linear functions, a 'rate of change' is the gradient of a straight-line graph.

The graph of °F against °C is a **temperature conversion graph** with °F on the vertical axis and °C on the horizontal axis.

Why 32° and 212°

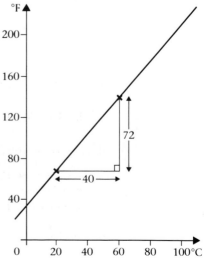

4

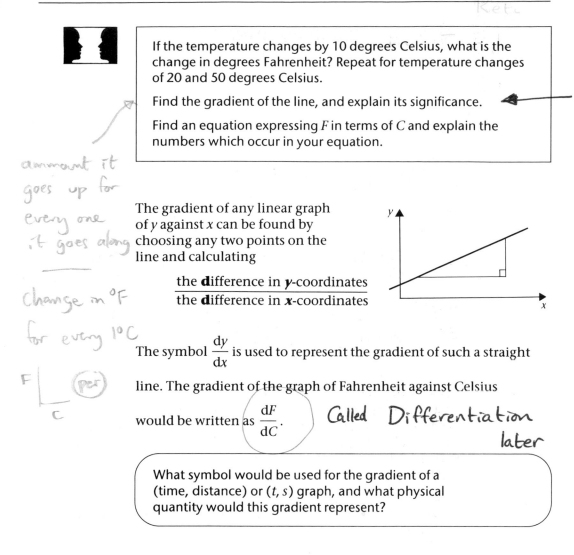

If the temperature changes by 10 degrees Celsius, what is the change in degrees Fahrenheit? Repeat for temperature changes of 20 and 50 degrees Celsius.

Find the gradient of the line, and explain its significance.

Find an equation expressing F in terms of C and explain the numbers which occur in your equation.

ammount it goes up for every one it goes along

Change in °F for every 1°C

The gradient of any linear graph of y against x can be found by choosing any two points on the line and calculating

$$\frac{\text{the \textbf{d}ifference in } y\text{-coordinates}}{\text{the \textbf{d}ifference in } x\text{-coordinates}}$$

The symbol $\dfrac{dy}{dx}$ is used to represent the gradient of such a straight

line. The gradient of the graph of Fahrenheit against Celsius

would be written as $\dfrac{dF}{dC}$.

Called Differentiation later

What symbol would be used for the gradient of a (time, distance) or (t, s) graph, and what physical quantity would this gradient represent?

EXERCISE 1

1 For the line with equation $y = 3x + 2$, copy and complete these statements.

(a) gradient of line =   (b) $\dfrac{dy}{dx} =$

2 For the graph of $y = 6 - 3x$

(a) what are the 'difference in y-coordinates' and the 'difference in x-coordinates' from A to B?

(b) Find $\dfrac{dy}{dx}$

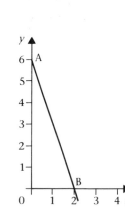

5

3 Write down the gradient, $\dfrac{dy}{dx}$, for each of the lines with equations

(a) $y = 5 - 7x$ (b) $y = 4 + x$

(c) $y = -2x$ (d) $y = \frac{1}{2}x - 1$

4 The graph of $2y + x = 4$ is as shown.

(a) What are the 'difference in y-coordinates' and the 'difference in x-coordinates' from A to B?

(b) Find $\dfrac{dy}{dx}$.

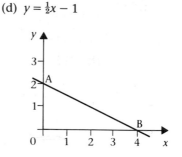

5 Write down the gradient, $\dfrac{dy}{dx}$, for each of the lines with equations

(a) $2y = x + 4$ (b) $y + x = 7$

(c) $x - y = 6$ (d) $2y + x = 4$

6 The cost of electricity consists of a standing charge of 702p and a charge of 2.87p for each unit of electricity used.

(a) Write the total cost, C pence, in terms of the number of units, n.

(b) Find $\dfrac{dC}{dn}$ and explain what it means.

7 Copy and complete:

(a) $s = 3 - 8t \;\Rightarrow\; \dfrac{ds}{dt} = \quad$ ($\Rightarrow$ is a symbol used for 'therefore'.)

(b) $y = 4t + 2 \;\Rightarrow$

(c) $z = 2 - y \;\Rightarrow$

(d) $y = 5(2x + 1) \;\Rightarrow\; y = 10x + 5$

$\Rightarrow \dfrac{dy}{dx} =$

(e) $y = 4(3 - 5x) \;\Rightarrow$

8 The circumference, C, of a circle of radius r is given by the formula $C = 2\pi r$.

(a) Find $\dfrac{dC}{dr}$. Explain what this rate of change represents.

(b) A wire is placed taut around the earth's equator. Approximately how much extra wire would be needed to enable the wire to be pulled 2 metres away from the surface at all points?

(c) Answer part (b) for a similar wire pulled taut around the moon.

1.2 Linear functions

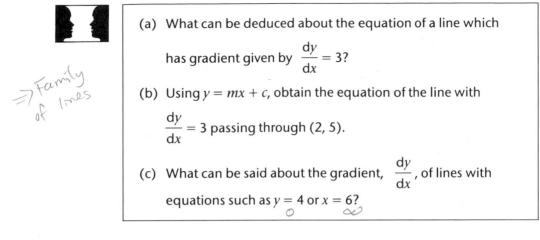

(a) What can be deduced about the equation of a line which has gradient given by $\dfrac{dy}{dx} = 3$?

(b) Using $y = mx + c$, obtain the equation of the line with $\dfrac{dy}{dx} = 3$ passing through (2, 5).

(c) What can be said about the gradient, $\dfrac{dy}{dx}$, of lines with equations such as $y = 4$ or $x = 6$?

→ Family of lines (handwritten annotation)

The area of mathematics known as the calculus was developed to enable mathematicians to tackle situations involving rates of change. This chapter will develop some ideas about rates of change for linear functions only; later chapters will extend these ideas to more general functions.

Here is a simple example involving connected rates of change:

A water heater is 95 cm high and has a cross-sectional area of 2700 cm². It is initially full of water.

As the bath is filled, the depth, h cm, of water in the heater drops by 15 cm every minute. The volume V cm³ of water remaining therefore drops by 2700×15 cm³ every minute.

After t minutes

$h = 95 - 15t$
$V = 2700(95 - 15t)$

Write down $\dfrac{dh}{dt}$ and $\dfrac{dV}{dt}$ and explain the simple relationship between these rates of change.

If $y = au$ $\dfrac{dy}{dx} = a\dfrac{du}{dx}$ (handwritten annotation)

TASKSHEET 1 — *Combined rates of change (page 11)*

> If u and v are linear functions of x, and a and b are any constants, then $y = au + bv$ is also a linear function of x and
>
> $$\frac{dy}{dx} = a\,\frac{du}{dx} + b\,\frac{dv}{dx}$$
>
> The rates of change of the parts are combined in this way to give the rate of change of the whole.

EXERCISE 2

1 A linear graph has $\dfrac{dy}{dx} = 5$ and passes through the point $(-1, 2)$. Find its equation.

2 Find the equation of each of the following lines:

(a) the line passing through $(3, 2)$ with $\dfrac{dy}{dx} = -2$;

(b) the line passing through $(4, 3)$ with $\dfrac{ds}{dt} = \dfrac{1}{2}$;

(c) the line passing through $(-6, -1)$ with $\dfrac{dp}{dx} = \dfrac{2}{3}$.

3 A line passes through the points $(1, 5)$ and $(4, 11)$. Find $\dfrac{dy}{dx}$ and the equation of the line.

4 (a) A plumber charges £5 for a call-out plus £7 per hour for labour.

  (i) Write the charge £C as a formula in terms of t, the number of hours taken to do the job.

  (ii) What is the value of $\dfrac{dC}{dt}$?

(b) Another plumber charges £6 per hour for labour, and for a job lasting 3 hours the bill is £26.

  (i) Write down the value of $\dfrac{dC}{dt}$.

  (ii) Hence obtain the charge £C as a formula in terms of t, the number of hours taken to do the job.

5   The marks obtained in a test ranged from 25 to 50. They have to be rescaled to range from 0 to 100. Copy and complete this table.

Test mark, T	25	26		50
Rescaled mark, R	0		96	100

(a) Find $\dfrac{\mathrm{d}R}{\mathrm{d}T}$.

(b) Hence express R in terms of T.

6   The growth of the population of Britain in the first half of the twentieth century was approximately linear, rising from roughly 38 million in 1900 to 48 million in 1950.

(a) Find an expression for the population P millions of people t years after 1900.

(b) Find $\dfrac{\mathrm{d}P}{\mathrm{d}t}$. What does it represent?

(c) What does your formula give for the population in 1990? Comment on your answer.

7   Let $u = 4 + 2x$ and $v = 5 - 4x$.

(a) Write down $\dfrac{\mathrm{d}u}{\mathrm{d}x}$ and $\dfrac{\mathrm{d}v}{\mathrm{d}x}$.

(b) Calculate $\dfrac{\mathrm{d}y}{\mathrm{d}x}$ for each of the following functions, **without** expressing y as a function of x.

    (i) $y = u + v$ (ii) $y = u - v$ (iii) $y = 3u + v$

    (iv) $y = u - 3v$ (v) $y = 3u + 2v$ (vi) $y = 2u - 3v$

(c) For each part of (b), substitute for u and v, then express y in terms of x. Hence check the value of $\dfrac{\mathrm{d}y}{\mathrm{d}x}$.

8   Making steamed puddings in a pressure cooker involves placing a basin containing a dough made from flour and suet into boiling water in a pressure cooker. To allow the raising agent to take effect, a short steaming time is allowed at low heat and then the cooker is brought to the appropriate pressure for the remaining cooking time.

One recipe for four portions recommends:

Amount of flour	Steaming time	Cooking time at pressure
200 grams	15 minutes	25 minutes

To adjust the recipe for other quantities, it is suggested that for every additional 15 grams of flour an extra 1 minute should be added to both the steaming time and the cooking time.

Let f grams be the amount of flour, s minutes the steaming time and p minutes the cooking time at pressure.

(a) Write s in terms of f. Hence find the value of $\dfrac{ds}{df}$ and describe the meaning in words of this rate of change.

(b) Write p in terms of f. Hence find the value of $\dfrac{dp}{df}$ and describe the meaning in words of this rate of change.

(c) Find T the total cooking time in minutes. Hence find the value of $\dfrac{dT}{df}$ and describe the meaning of this rate of change.

After working through this chapter you should, for linear functions:

1 know that $\dfrac{du}{dv}$ is the notation for the gradient of the graph of u against v;

2 for equations such as $y = 5 - 2z$, be able to write down the rate of change, $\dfrac{dy}{dz} = -2$;

3 be familiar with the result that, if u, v are linear functions of x with a, b any constants, then $y = au + bv$ is also a linear function and

$$\frac{dy}{dx} = a\,\frac{du}{dx} + b\,\frac{dv}{dx}$$

(i.e. the rates of change of the parts are combined in this way to give the rate of change of the whole);

4 be able to find and apply rates of change in simple problems.

Combined rates of change

Do Q4 with.

1 A handbook issued with a microwave oven gives the following guide for cooking a whole chicken from frozen.

'Thaw on a low setting for 15 minutes per kilogram, then stand in cold water for 30 minutes. Next cook on a high setting for 20 minutes per kilogram, then let it stand for 16 minutes.'

Consider a chicken of weight w kg, so that the time taken in minutes for the first stage is $u = 15w + 30$.

(a) Write down a similar formula for v, the time in minutes for the second stage.

(b) Hence find an expression for the total time taken, $T = u + v$, in terms of w.

        Stage 1   2   Total

(c) Write down the values of $\dfrac{du}{dw}, \dfrac{dv}{dw}$ and $\dfrac{dT}{dw}$. What do these rates of change represent?

    extra number of minutes / kilogram

(d) Explain why $\dfrac{dT}{dw} = \dfrac{du}{dw} + \dfrac{dv}{dw}$.

   Add the extra times for each stage

2 In a running club, training is sometimes carried out in pairs. The faster runner remains at the start, while the slower one moves 200 metres forward. They then start running simultaneously and the time taken for the slower runner to be caught is measured.

Consider one particular pair of runners whose speeds are $8\,\mathrm{m\,s^{-1}}$ and $6\,\mathrm{m\,s^{-1}}$. Let f denote the distance in metres of the *faster* runner from the start and s the distance of the *slower* runner from the start, t seconds after they both start running.

Write down formulas for f and s in terms of t. Hence find an expression for $x = s - f$ in terms of t. Explain what x represents. — *distance*

Write down the values of $\dfrac{df}{dt}, \dfrac{ds}{dt}$ and $\dfrac{dx}{dt}$. Explain what these rates of change represent and describe and explain a simple relationship between them.

3 Let $u = 3x + 1$ and $v = 2x - 3$.

(a) Write down the values of $\dfrac{du}{dx}$ and $\dfrac{dv}{dx}$.

(b) By substituting for u and v, find an expression for y in terms of x for each of the following:

(i) $y = u + v$ (ii) $y = 2u + v$

(iii) $y = u - v$ (iv) $y = 4u - 3v$

(c) For each part of (b) write down the value of $\dfrac{dy}{dx}$.

(d) State the relationship between $\dfrac{du}{dx}$, $\dfrac{dv}{dx}$ and $\dfrac{dy}{dx}$ in each case.

linear combination

(e) What would the relationship be if $y = au + bv$, where a, b are constants?

4 (a) A firm charges a basic fee of £12 plus £5 per hour for each engineer sent out on repair work. If one engineer is called out for t hours, write down an expression for u, the charge in £, in terms of t.

(b) A rival firm charges a basic fee of £9 plus £6 per hour for each engineer sent. Write down an expression for the charge £v if one engineer is called out for t hours.

(c) Comment on which firm is cheaper.

(d) Write down $\dfrac{du}{dt}$ and $\dfrac{dv}{dt}$ and explain their significance.

(e) In an emergency, a factory calls out three engineers from the first firm and two from the second. Write the total cost £c in terms of u and v.

(f) Deduce the value of $\dfrac{dc}{dt}$ and explain its meaning.

2 Gradients of curves

2.1 Locally straight curves

> The diagram shows the positions of four skiers A, B, C and D on a snow-covered hill. Note down some similarities and some differences between the four skiers.

You have already investigated the gradients of straight lines. For a curve, the gradient itself changes as you move along the curve. It is therefore called the **gradient at a point**.

Imagine looking through a telescope at the skier at point B.

> Use the picture to estimate the gradient of the hill at this point.

It is possible to use a computer to enlarge portions of a graph, effectively zooming-in to a curve and showing its shape near a chosen point.

TASKSHEET 1 — Zoom! (page 25)

> If a curve appears to be a straight line when you zoom in at a point, then it is 'locally straight' at that point.

On tasksheet 1, when you zoomed in on graphs you found that some functions, such as $y = |x|$, were not 'locally straight' everywhere. For example, the graph of $y = |x^2 - 4|$ is locally straight at all points **except** $(2, 0)$ and $(-2, 0)$.

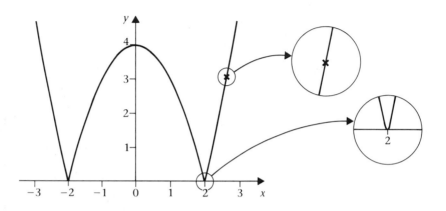

However, the cubic graph **was** locally straight everywhere. In fact, so are **all** polynomial graphs. Suppose you could superimpose the telescopic view of the skier onto the view of the hill at a particular point. Considering just the skis and the slope, you would see the following:

The skis form what is called a **tangent** to the curve.

> When you zoom in, how is the local straight line that you see related to the tangent line?

> The gradient of a curve at a point is the same as the gradient of the tangent to the curve at that point.

14

2.2 Obtaining a gradient

You are already able to state some gradients **exactly**. For example,

$$y = 5x + 4 \implies \frac{dy}{dx} = 5$$

For non-linear graphs the notation $\frac{dy}{dx}$ is still used, but now this represents

the **d**ifference between y-coordinates
---
the **d**ifference between x-coordinates

along the tangent at the point P.

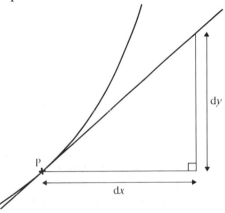

The process of obtaining $\frac{dy}{dx}$ for a given function y of x is called **differentiation**.

A practical method for measuring $\frac{dy}{dx}$ at any point on a curve is introduced on tasksheet 2.

Needs grad. meas.

TASKSHEET 2 – *Measuring gradients (page 27)* + *Data sheets 1, 2, 3*

＊ ⟨ERROR⟩

The gradient measurer enables you to obtain the gradient, $\frac{dy}{dx}$,

at a point on a curve. Plotting the values of the gradient against x produces a graph called the gradient graph. The relationship between a graph and its gradient graph forms the subject of the remaining sections of this chapter.

2.3 Gradient graphs

The previous section showed that the value of the gradient changes for different points on a graph. On the graph shown below, the imaginary skier would experience:

- a numerically large negative gradient which increases to zero at A;

- a positive gradient which increases from A to B and then decreases to zero at C;

- a gradient which finally decreases through numerically larger and larger negative values.

If you plot the gradient at each point against *x*, you obtain (very roughly) a **gradient graph** as shown.

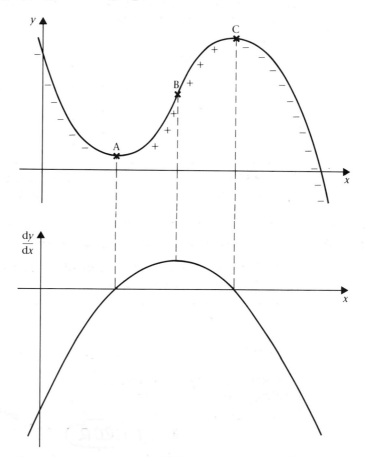

A, B and C are special points; A and C are the only points where the gradient is zero and B is the point where the gradient is maximum.

 TASKSHEET 3 — Gradient graphs (page 28)   Program for graphic Calculator (technology datasheets)

Formulas?

Points of a graph where the curve has zero gradient are called **stationary points.**

Points where a graph is locally a maximum or minimum are called **turning points**.

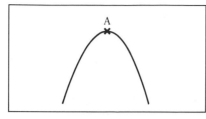

This **local maximum** is both a stationary point and a turning point.

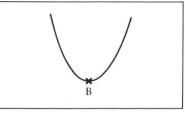

This is a **local minimum**.

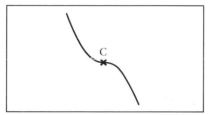

This is a stationary point but not a turning point.

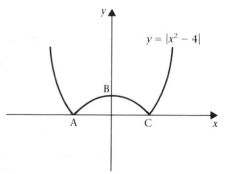

This is a turning point but not a stationary point.

(a) Explain why D is not a stationary point.

(b) Why do you think the word (**local**) is used for the maximum and minimum points above?

EXAMPLE 1

Find the stationary points and/or turning points on the graph of

$$y = |x^2 - 4|$$

$y = |x^2 - 4|$

SOLUTION

A and C are turning points (local minima) but are not stationary points. B is both a stationary point and a turning point (a local maximum).

Early?

CHECK PLACE IN FOUNDATIONS.

17

2.4 Equations of gradient graphs

On tasksheet 2, you should have found that the graph of $y = \frac{1}{2}x^2$ has a gradient graph with $\dfrac{dy}{dx} = x$ as its equation.

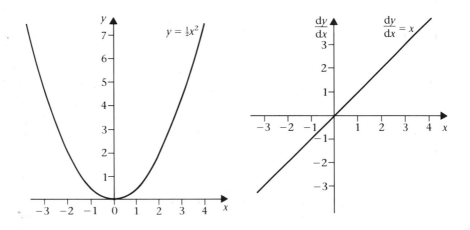

The gradient measurer can be used to determine quite accurately the gradient graphs for other quadratics.

TASKSHEET 4 – Quadratics (page 30)

You have seen some justification for the following result:

$$y = ax^2 + c \;\Rightarrow\; \frac{dy}{dx} = 2ax$$

EXAMPLE 2

Find the gradient of the graph of $y = 3x^2 + 1$ when $x = 2$.

SOLUTION

$$y = 3x^2 + 1 \;\Rightarrow\; \frac{dy}{dx} = 6x$$

At $x = 2$, the gradient is 12.

2.5 Finding gradients numerically

The gradient of a graph at a given point can be obtained very accurately using a microcomputer or calculator.

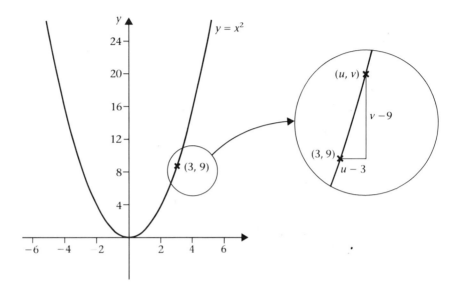

If you zoom in at (3, 9), you know the property of local straightness will mean that the graph looks increasingly like a straight line which becomes more and more like the tangent to the graph at (3, 9). So, to find the gradient of the tangent, you can use the curve itself.

> (a) How close should (u, v) be to (3, 9)?
>
> (b) Suggest coordinates for (u, v).

Using (u, v) you will get an approximate gradient for $y = x^2$ at $x = 3$ by calculating

$$\text{approximate gradient} = \frac{v - 9}{u - 3}$$

Why does this give only an approximation?

How could you obtain a better approximation to the actual gradient?

Obtain a value for the gradient using a calculator or computer. Details are given on technology datasheet: *Calculating gradients*.

It is often convenient to use function notation when finding gradients numerically.

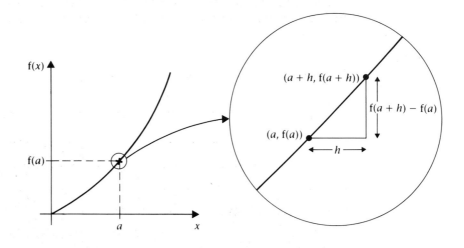

The gradient of the graph of a function f(x) at a point $(a, f(a))$ is given the symbol f'(a), and can be estimated numerically as

$$f'(a) \approx \frac{f(a + h) - f(a)}{h} \qquad \frac{\delta y}{\delta x}$$

where h, the difference in x, is small.

EXAMPLE 3

Find the gradient of the graph of $f(x) = 2x^3 - 3x^2$ at $(2, 4)$.

SOLUTION

$f(2) = 4$ and $f(2.00001) = 4.000\,120\,001\ldots$

and so the gradient of the graph is approximately

$$f'(2) \approx \frac{4.000\,120\,001 - 4}{0.00001} = 12.0001$$

Using smaller differences in x will result in values closer and closer to 12. This limit is the gradient of the graph.

If $f(x) = 2x^3 - 3x^2$ then f'$(2) = 12$.

20

2.6 **Gradient functions**

The great speed and accuracy of numerical methods, compared with the use of the gradient measurer, enables you to construct many gradient functions.

TASKSHEET 5 — Gradient functions (page 31)

The tasksheet gave considerable evidence for the following result.

> A polynomial graph with equation of the form
>
> $$y = a + bx + cx^2 + dx^3$$
>
> has a gradient graph with equation
>
> $$\frac{dy}{dx} = b + 2cx + 3dx^2$$

$\dfrac{dy}{dx}$ is called the **derivative** of y with respect to x and

$b + 2cx + 3dx^2$ is called the **derived function**.

EXAMPLE 4

(a) Find the gradient of the graph of $y = 1 - 3x + 2x^2$ at the point $(2, 3)$.

(b) Hence find the equation of the tangent at $(2, 3)$.

SOLUTION

(a) $\dfrac{dy}{dx} = -3 + 4x$. At the point $(2, 3)$, $\dfrac{dy}{dx} = -3 + 4 \times 2 = 5$

(b) The tangent has gradient 5 and passes through $(2, 3)$. If (x, y) is any other point on the tangent, then

$$\frac{y - 3}{x - 2} = 5 \implies y - 3 = 5x - 10 \implies y = 5x - 7$$

The equation of the tangent is $y = 5x - 7$.

EXERCISE 1

1   Use the rules you have discovered to find the equation of the gradient graph for each of the following.

(a) $y = 3x^2 + 4$ (b) $v = 5u^3 - 2u^2$

(c) $y = 6 - x^2$ (d) $s = 4t - t^2$

2   For the graph whose equation is $y = 2 + 5x^2$,

(a) write down the equation of the gradient graph;

(b) write down the gradients of the graph at

(i) $(1, 7)$ (ii) $(2, 22)$ (iii) the point where $x = -1$.

Follow Ex 3.

3   Find the gradients of each of the following graphs at the given points.

(a) $y = 3 - 2x^3$ at $(0, 3)$ and $(2, -13)$

(b) $y = 5x - x^2$ at $(2, 6)$ and $(4, 4)$

4   Find the equations of the tangents to each of the following graphs at $(2, 3)$.

(a) $y = 3 + 2x - x^2$

(b) $y = x^3 - 5$

(c) $y = 7 + x^2 - x^3$

5   Find the equation of the tangent to $y = x + 2x^2$ at the point whose x-coordinate is 3.

6   Find the equations of the tangents to each of the following graphs at $(0, 5)$.

(a) $y = 5 + x - x^3$

(b) $y = 5 - 3x + 2x^3$

(c) $y = 5 + 4x^2 + 3x^3$

TASKSHEET 6E   –   *Tangents and normals (page 33)*

Perpendicular lines

2.7 Leibnitz notation

Calculus is the study of the changes of a continuously varying function. In this chapter, you have looked at the gradients of locally straight curves and, in particular, the gradients of graphs of polynomial functions. At any point, the gradient of a locally straight curve is the same as the gradient of its tangent at that point. The concept of a derivative arose chiefly as the result of many centuries of effort spent in drawing tangents to curves and finding the velocities of bodies in non-uniform motion.

Isaac Newton was born in 1642 and entered Cambridge University in 1660, quickly mastering all the mathematics known at that time. In 1665, the year of the Great Plague, he invented his 'method of fluxions', which was a method of dealing with varying quantities. If a quantity, say x, was a function of time t, then Newton used the notation $\dot{x}$ to represent $\dfrac{dx}{dt}$. In mechanics, the notations $\dot{x}$ and $\dot{y}$ are still used to represent velocities in the x and y directions respectively. During the Great Plague, Newton retired from Cambridge to his home in Lincolnshire. There, he investigated various applications of his method, including finding the equations of tangents. His treatise on calculus was written in 1671 but its publication did not take place until 1736, nine years after his death. It is interesting that in his *Principia* of 1687, in which he dealt with both terrestrial and celestial mechanics, he relied on geometry and did not use fluxions.

Because Newton's results were published so late, a bitter controversy arose between the supporters of Newton and the German mathematician and philosopher, Leibnitz. Gottfried Leibnitz (1646–1716) had not yet started his study of mathematics in 1671 and it was not until 29 October 1675 that the first mention of the calculus notation in use today appeared in his notes. Having noticed that differentiation reduced the degree of a polynomial, he used the notation $\dfrac{x}{d}$ but soon changed this to dx. In 1676, in correspondence with the Royal Society, Leibnitz learnt that Newton had produced some important results. Newton supplied him with a variety of theorems but referred to his method of fluxions by means of two anagrams from which Leibnitz deduced nothing. In a reply he gave his rules for dy and dx. Newton, in his *Principia*, mentioned that Leibnitz had discovered independently a method 'which hardly differed from mine except in words and symbols'.

The greatest merit of Leibnitz's work was his creation of a mathematical symbolism. Besides his introduction of dx, he invented the notations $\frac{dy}{dx}$ and $\frac{d}{dx}$.

In the text you have seen that $\frac{dy}{dx}$ represents

$$\frac{\text{the difference in } y\text{- coordinates}}{\text{the difference in } x\text{-coordinates}}$$

along the tangent to the curve. Using the notation invented by Leibnitz,

$$y = 2x^3 \;\Rightarrow\; \frac{dy}{dx} = 6x^2 \quad \text{or} \quad \frac{d}{dx}(2x^3) = 6x^2$$

$$f'(x) = 6x^2$$

After working through this chapter you should:

1 be able to use the gradient measurer or microcomputer to find gradients for graphs which are locally straight;

2 be able to sketch the gradient graph for a given graph;

3 know that
$$y = a + bx + cx^2 + dx^3 \;\Rightarrow\; \frac{dy}{dx} = b + 2cx + 3dx^2$$

4 recognise the rule above for differentiating cubics as a particular case of a general rule (not yet proved) that if a, b are constants and u, v are functions of x, then
$$y = au + bv \;\Rightarrow\; \frac{dy}{dx} = a\frac{du}{dx} + b\frac{dv}{dx}$$

5 be able to find the equation of a tangent to a graph at a given point.

Zoom!

This tasksheet requires the use of a microcomputer or graphical calculator to enlarge and zoom in on a part of a graph. Help is given on technology datasheet: *Zoom*.

1 (a) Input the graph of $y = x^3 - 7x^2 + 8x + 7$ for $0 \leq x \leq 5$.

   (b) Zoom in to the point with $x = 2$ and redraw.

   (c) Repeat, increasing the magnification. What do you notice?

When you zoom in at some point on a sufficiently smooth curve, the curve starts to look more and more like a straight line. The diagram below shows this for the graph $y = x^2 - 2$.

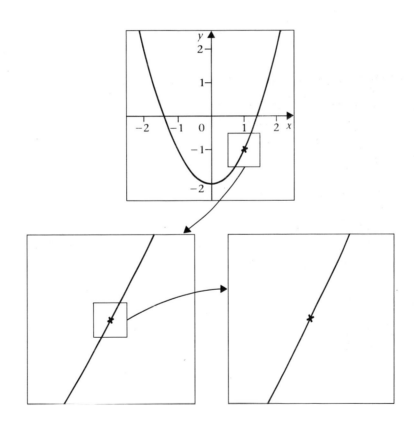

2 (a) What would you expect to see if you zoomed in at $(0, -2)$ on the graph $y = x^2 - 2$?

   (b) Check your answer on the graph plotter.

3   (a) Plot the graph $y = x^3 - 7x^2 + 8x + 7$. What would you expect to see if you zoomed in at $x = 4$?

   (b) Zoom in and check your answer to (a).

   (c) Where else would this graph look the same when you zoom in?

4   Investigate the local straightness of the following graphs.

   (a) $y = |x|$ ($|x|$ is entered on some graph plotters as ABS(x).)

   (b) $y = 100x^2$ (c) $y = \text{Int}(x)$ (d) $y = |x^2 - 4|$

5E (a) Use the graph plotter to obtain the graph of $y = \frac{1}{5}\sin 3x$. Describe fully in words the transformations from the graph of $y = \sin x$ to that of $y = \frac{1}{5}\sin 3x$.

   (b) Use the graph plotter to obtain the graph of

      (i) $y = \sin x + \frac{1}{5}\sin 3x$

      (ii) $y = \sin x + \frac{1}{50}\sin 100x$ (Use *Zoom* to investigate this graph.)

   (c) Can you invent a function whose graph looks just like that of $y = \sin x$ under normal magnification but not under magnification $\times 1000$?

Measuring gradients

For this worksheet you will need the gradient measurer. Instructions for its use are on technology datasheet: *Measuring gradients.* You will also need datasheets 1, 2 and 3.

1 For this question you will need datasheet 1, which shows the graph of $y = \frac{1}{2}x^2$.

(a) Measure the gradient $\dfrac{dy}{dx}$ of the curve at the point (1.5, 1.125).

(b) Measure the gradients of the curve at

(i) (1, 0.5)   (ii) (2, 2)   (iii) (3, 4.5)

(c) Measure the gradient, $\dfrac{dy}{dx}$, of the curve at the point $(-2, 2)$.

(d) What is the gradient of the curve at   (i) $(-1, 0.5)$,   (ii) $(-3, 4.5)$?

(e) Using your answers to previous parts of this question, plot all the

points $\left(x, \dfrac{dy}{dx}\right)$. Join them up to obtain a gradient graph. Complete the

equation $\dfrac{dy}{dx} =$

refer to datasheet 2 (cubic)

2 (a) ~~What would you expect to see if you zoomed in at (0, −2) on the graph~~
~~$y = x^2 - 2$?~~   *(a) Measure grad at number of points (integer values)*
~~(b) Check your answer on the graph plotter.~~

(b) Mark the points $\left(x, \dfrac{dy}{dx}\right)$ on a set of axes and sketch the resulting graph.

(c) The original graph has a cubic equation. What type of equation does the gradient graph appear to have?

3 For this question you will need datasheet 3, which shows the graph of $y = 21 + 4x - x^2$.

(a) Measure the gradient at a number of different points on the curve.

(b) Check that your answers satisfy the equation of the gradient graph $\dfrac{dy}{dx} = 4 - 2x$.

Gradient graphs

1 Copy each of these graphs. Directly beneath each one, sketch the corresponding gradient graph, using the same scale for x.

Mark any points you think are special and state the important features of each graph.

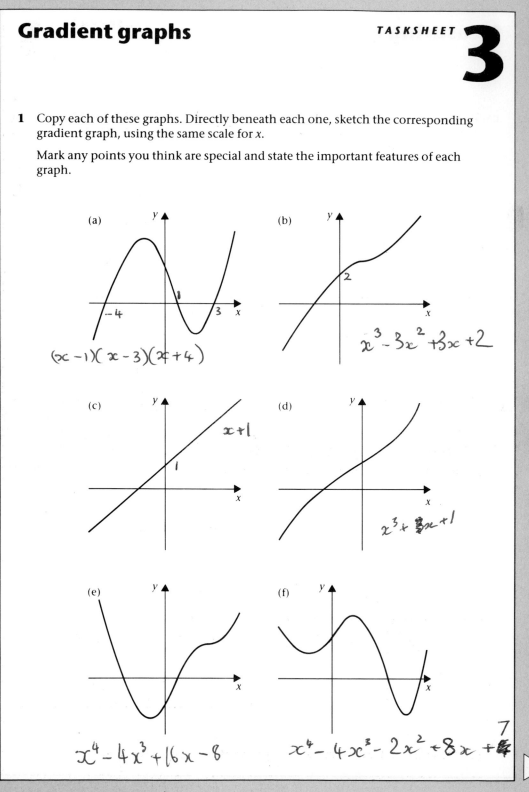

(a)

$(x-1)(x-3)(x+4)$

(b)

$x^3 - 3x^2 + 3x + 2$

(c)

$x + 1$

(d)

$x^3 + \frac{3}{2}x + 1$

(e)

$x^4 - 4x^3 + 16x - 8$

(f)

$x^4 - 4x^3 - 2x^2 + 8x + \frac{7}{4}$

$(x+4)(x-2)$

2 Sketch each of these graphs and its gradient graph. Start by deciding what happens to each gradient graph when x is near zero and also when x is numerically large (either positive or negative).

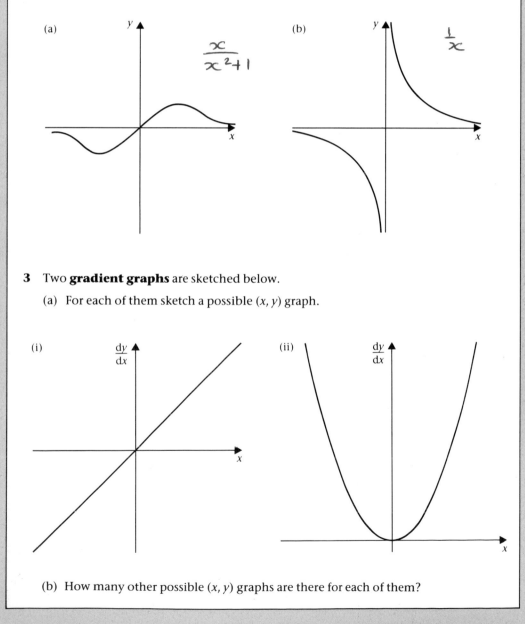

(a) $$\frac{x}{x^2+1}$$

(b) $$\frac{1}{x}$$

3 Two **gradient graphs** are sketched below.

(a) For each of them sketch a possible (x, y) graph.

(i) $\frac{dy}{dx}$

(ii) $\frac{dy}{dx}$

(b) How many other possible (x, y) graphs are there for each of them?

Quadratics

For this tasksheet you will need the gradient measurer. Instructions for its use are on technology datasheet: *Measuring gradients.* You will also need three copies of datasheet 4.

1 (a) For the graph of $y = \frac{1}{2}x^2 + 1$, mark and label axes on datasheet 4. Let 1 unit be represented by 2 cm on each axis.

   (b) Use the gradient measurer to confirm that $\dfrac{dy}{dx} = 2$ at the point (2, 3).

   (c) Use the gradient measurer to find sufficient gradients to sketch the gradient graph, and state its equation.

   (d) How are the graphs of $y = \frac{1}{2}x^2 + 1$, $y = \frac{1}{2}x^2 - 2$ and, generally, $y = \frac{1}{2}x^2 + c$ all related to that of $y = \frac{1}{2}x^2$?

   (e) What can be deduced about the gradient graph for any curve of the form $y = \frac{1}{2}x^2 + c$?

2 (a) For the graph of $y = x^2$, mark and label axes on a new copy of datasheet 4. Let 1 unit be represented by 4 cm on each axis.

   (b) Use the gradient measurer to find sufficient gradients to sketch the gradient graph, and state its equation.

   (c) Carefully explain why the gradient of $y = x^2$ is twice that of $y = \frac{1}{2}x^2$ for corresponding values of x.

   (d) What would you expect the gradient graph for $y = 3x^2$ to be? Use another copy of datasheet 4 to check your result. Remember that the graph passes through (0, 0) and (1, 3), so you will need to be careful when scaling the axes and using the gradient measurer.

   (e) What can be deduced about the gradient graph for any curve of the form $y = ax^2$?

3 What is the equation of the gradient graph of $y = ax^2 + c$?

Gradient functions

Computer Version

TASKSHEET **5**

For this tasksheet you may need technology datasheet: *Gradient graphs*.

1

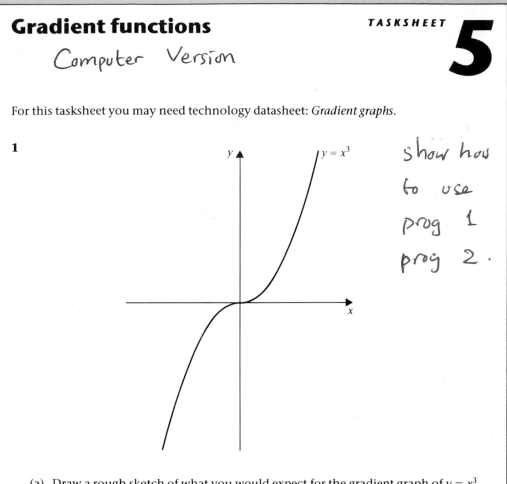

$y = x^3$

show how
to use
prog 1
prog 2.

(a) Draw a rough sketch of what you would expect for the gradient graph of $y = x^3$.

(b) Use a <u>numerical method</u> to calculate the gradient at $x = 0, 1, -2$ and 3.

(c) What is the gradient function?

Many graph plotters will calculate gradients numerically for several values of x and plot them on the graph. This gives you an accurate picture of the gradient graph. You can then make a sensible guess at the equation of the gradient graph and check your conjecture by superimposing. Use a graph plotter with this facility to check your answer to question 1(c) and to answer the rest of this tasksheet.

2   For a function of the form

$$y = ax^3$$

what does the gradient function appear to be?

A general polynomial is built up from multiples of simple powers of x. For example, $x + x^2$ is built up as shown below:

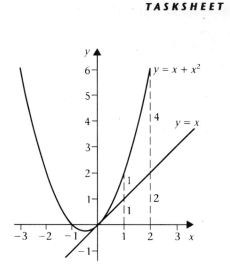

x	0	1	2	3
x^2	0	1	4	9
$x + x^2$	0	2	6	12

When x increases from 1 to 2, x increases by 1, x^2 increases by 3 and $x + x^2$ increases by both amounts, i.e. 4.

Does this remind you of a result you discovered in *Rates of change*?

In *Rates of change* you found that if $y = au + bv$, where u, v are linear functions of x, then

$$\frac{dy}{dx} = a\frac{du}{dx} + b\frac{dv}{dx}$$

You might expect functions that are locally straight to behave in a similar way to linear functions.

on computer (superimpose)

(3) If $y = ax + bx^2$, check that $\dfrac{dy}{dx} = a + 2bx$ for various values of a and b.

4 If $y = a + bx + cx^2 + dx^3$, find the equation of the gradient graph.

5E If $y = ax^n + bx^m$, find the gradient function.

Tangents and normals

A line with gradient $-\frac{1}{2}$ makes a right angle with a line with gradient 2.

Each line is said to be **normal** to the other.

1 If a line is drawn with a gradient g, what can you say about the gradient of a line which is normal to it?

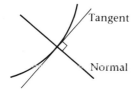

A line is said to be a normal to a curve at a given point if it is normal to the tangent at that point.

2 The graph of $y = \frac{1}{3}x^3$ has tangents drawn at $x = 1$ and at $x = -1$. These two tangents and the normals to the tangents form a rectangle.

 (a) Sketch the graph with the tangents and normals shown.

 (b) Find the equations of the two tangents.

 (c) Find the equations of the two normals.

 (d) Use your answers to (b) and (c) to find the coordinates of all four corners of the rectangle.

 (e) What is the area of the rectangle?

3 Tangents and normals drawn on the graph of $y = x^2$ form a square as shown.

 (a) Find the coordinates of the four corners of the square.

 (b) Show that the area of the square is $\frac{1}{2}$.

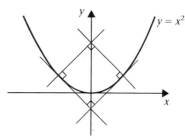

4

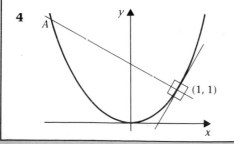

The normal to the graph of $y = x^2$ at $(1, 1)$ cuts the graph at A as shown.

Find A.

3 Optimisation

3.1 Graphs and gradient graphs

Optimisation is the process of producing the most favourable
outcome: the greatest food supply or the least pollution, for
example. Decision-making can sometimes depend upon an analysis
using calculus and stationary points. Before tackling such
optimisation problems we shall review the use of stationary points
in graph sketching.

Part of the graph of

$$y = x^3 - 2x^2 + x + 1$$

is as sketched.

(a) Explain how the details of the graph shown above are
    obtained.

(b) What features of the $\left(x, \dfrac{dy}{dx}\right)$ gradient graph as sketched
    below can you relate to the shape of the (x, y) graph?

(c) How are the gaps completed for this graph?
    How can you be certain that your sketch is roughly correct?

The graph of

$$\frac{dy}{dx} = 3x^2 - 4x + 1$$

is shown here.

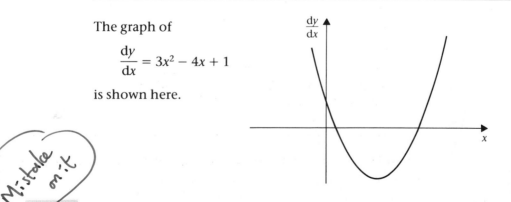

TASKSHEET 1 — Graph sketching (page 44)

34

The values and behaviour of $\dfrac{dy}{dx}$ can be used to help sketch graphs.

> Knowing the gradient of a graph at a point tells you what the graph is like **near the point** and not just at the point itself.
>
> Finding the stationary points (where $\dfrac{dy}{dx} = 0$) can help you to determine quickly the overall shape of the graph.

EXAMPLE 1

(a) Sketch the graph of $y = x^2 - 5x$.

(b) Indicate on your sketch where $\dfrac{dy}{dx}$ is positive and where it is negative.

(c) For what value of x does $\dfrac{dy}{dx} = 0$?

(d) Is this point a maximum or a minimum? State its coordinates.

SOLUTION

(a) $y = x^2 - 5x$ or $y = x(x - 5)$

(b) $+, -,$ as on the graph

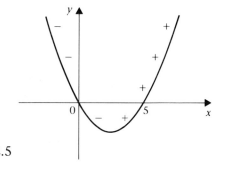

(c) $y = x^2 - 5x \Rightarrow \dfrac{dy}{dx} = 2x - 5$

$\dfrac{dy}{dx} = 0 \Rightarrow 2x - 5 = 0 \Rightarrow x = 2.5$

(d) It is clear from the graph that it is a **minimum**.
When $x = 2.5$, $y = 2.5^2 - 5 \times 2.5 = -6.25$.
The coordinates are $(2.5, -6.25)$.

> In (a), how do you know that the quadratic curve is not the other way up?
>
> Carefully justify the alternative solution to (c): $x = \dfrac{0 + 5}{2} = 2.5$

EXERCISE 1

1   Sketch $y = (x - 1)(x - 2)(x - 4)$. What extra information about the graph could be obtained using calculus? (There is no need to find this extra information!)

2   Three cubic graphs are sketched below.

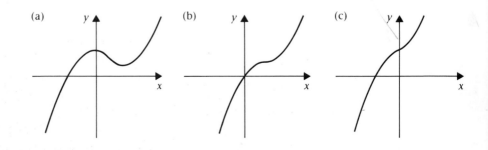

Sketch the corresponding $\left(x, \dfrac{dy}{dx} \right)$ graphs and relate features of the gradient graphs to the shape of the (x, y) graphs.

3   A cubic graph passes through $(0, 2)$ and has gradient graph as shown.

Sketch the (x, y) graph.

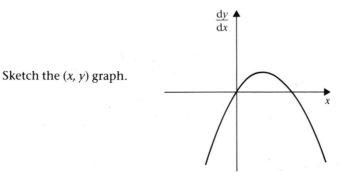

4   The distance travelled by an object in time t is given by
$$s = t^3 - 6t^2 + 12t$$

(a) Find $\dfrac{ds}{dt}$ and sketch the graph of $\dfrac{ds}{dt}$ against t.

(b) Sketch the graph of s against t.

(c) By considering the two graphs, describe the motion of the object.

3.2 Quadratics and cubics

It is easy to differentiate quadratic and cubic functions and hence to find the stationary points. The next tasksheet contains some examples of such functions.

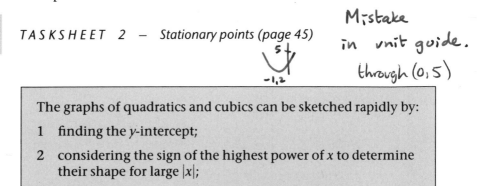

TASKSHEET 2 — Stationary points (page 45)

Mistake in unit guide.
through (0, 5)

The graphs of quadratics and cubics can be sketched rapidly by:

1 finding the y-intercept;

2 considering the sign of the highest power of x to determine their shape for large $|x|$;

3 finding the x-coordinates of any stationary points by solving the equation

$$\frac{dy}{dx} = 0$$

EXAMPLE 2

Sketch $y = -x^3 + 27x - 2$.

SOLUTION

For large x, the graph has roughly the same shape as that of $-x^3$.

At the stationary points,

$$\frac{dy}{dx} = 0$$
$$-3x^2 + 27 = 0$$
$$3(9 - x^2) = 0$$
$$x = 3 \text{ or } -3$$

When $x = 3$
$$y = -3^3 + 27 \times 3 - 2 = 52$$

When $x = -3$
$$y = -(-3)^3 + 27 \times (-3) - 2 = -56$$

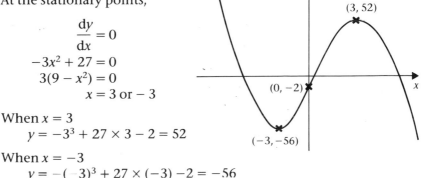

EXERCISE 2

1 The sketch shows the graph of $y = x^3 - 12x + 5$. Find the stationary points and hence draw in the axes on a copy of the sketch.

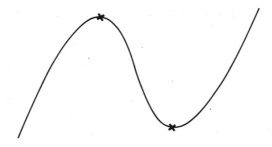

2 Repeat question 1 if the graph is that of $y = 2x^3 - 9x^2 + 12x - 7$.

3 For each function (a) to (f):

(i) find all the values of x, if any, for which $\dfrac{dy}{dx} = 0$ and sketch the graph;

(ii) find the coordinates of all the local maximum and minimum points;

(iii) indicate on your sketch the parts of the graphs where $\dfrac{dy}{dx}$ is positive and the parts where $\dfrac{dy}{dx}$ is negative.

Mistake.
⟹

(a) $y = 5x - x^2$ (b) $y = (1 - x)^2$

(c) $y = x^3 - 3x^2 + 5$ (d) $y = 4x - x^2 - 4$

(e) $y = 2x^3 - 9x^2 + 12$ (f) $y = x^4 - 8x^2 + 12$

4 The sketch graphs are those of $y = x^2 - 6x$ and $y = x^3 - 6x^2$.

(a) Find the x-coordinates of A, B and C. Explain the relationship between the x-coordinate of B and the other two x-coordinates.

(b) Find the x-coordinates of D, E and F. Does the relationship you noticed in (a) hold for this graph?

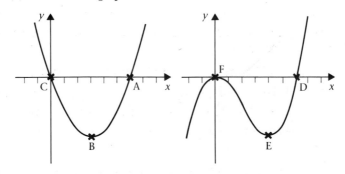

3.3 Maxima and minima

Cake Containers

Decision-making often depends upon choosing the value of one variable so as to maximise or minimise another variable. For example, it might involve maximising profits, minimising the amount of material used in a design, maximising the number of customers served each hour and so on. Calculus can be of great help in this decision-making process. The stages in such a process can be seen in the following simple example.

A circular piece of paper is folded into a cylindrical paper case for a cake. Where should the paper be folded to create the container of greatest volume?

> Without doing any calculations, write down what you think happens to the volume of the cylinder as it changes from a tall thin cylinder to a short fat cylinder as shown below.
>
> Draw a rough sketch of a graph which shows these changes in volume.

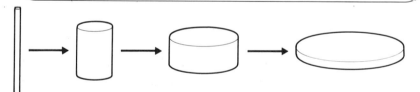

To use calculus methods to solve this problem you can express the volume, *V*, in terms of a suitable variable length.

V. Difficult

> Construct a formula for the volume *V* in terms of a chosen variable.
>
> Use calculus to find the maximum volume.
>
> What simplifying assumptions have you made in obtaining your answer? How reasonable are these assumptions?

TASKSHEET 3 — Using stationary points (page 46)

EXAMPLE 3

During a promotion drive, an electrical retailer sells a particular make of television at cost price. She finds that, at this price, she sells twenty televisions a week. However, according to a market survey the demand would fall to zero if the price were increased by £40.

By what amount should the retailer increase the price to make the maximum weekly profit?

SOLUTION

For a price increase of £I you can model the number sold by $N = 20 - \frac{1}{2}I$.

Explain this modelling assumption.

£I is the increase above cost price and so the profit (in £) is

$$P = NI$$
$$= (20 - \tfrac{1}{2}I)I$$
$$= 20I - \tfrac{1}{2}I^2$$

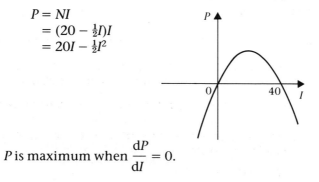

P is maximum when $\dfrac{\mathrm{d}P}{\mathrm{d}I} = 0$.

Since $\dfrac{\mathrm{d}P}{\mathrm{d}I} = 20 - I$, $\dfrac{\mathrm{d}P}{\mathrm{d}I} = 0$ when $I = 20$.

The retailer should increase the price by £20.

EXERCISE 3

1   The fuel consumption of a new car was measured when it was test driven at various speeds in top gear. For a speed of v miles per hour, the fuel consumption, f miles per gallon, was found to be roughly modelled, for $30 \leq v \leq 80$, by the formula $f = 25 + v - 0.012v^2$.

(a) Find f and $\dfrac{df}{dv}$ when $v = 35$ and when $v = 60$. What do these results indicate about fuel economy?

(b) What speed is most economical for this car?

2   As a result of a survey, the marketing director of a company found that the demand for its product was given approximately by the linear equation $n = 30 - 2P$ where n is the demand, or the number of items that will be sold (in millions), at a price £P.

If n million are sold at £P each then the revenue (money taken) will be £R million where

$$R = nP = (30 - 2P)P = 30P - 2P^2$$

(a) Find $\dfrac{dR}{dP}$ and explain what it means.

(b) Calculate the value of $\dfrac{dR}{dP}$ when $P = 5$ and when $P = 10$.

(c) For what selling prices is revenue rising?

(d) What is the best selling price? What is $\dfrac{dR}{dP}$ at this price?

Lead into next section

Use Paper A4

3   A rectangular strip of plastic of width 20 cm is folded into a length of guttering as shown.

Where should the folds be located to enable the gutter to carry as much water as possible?

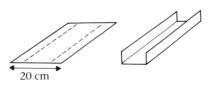

20 cm

4   A new housing estate started with a population of approximately 500 people.

(a) It was planned that it should grow by roughly 100 inhabitants each year. Find an expression for the intended population P of the estate t years after its opening. Find $\dfrac{dP}{dt}$ and explain what it represents.

(b) For various reasons, the new estate did not grow as planned and the population was better modelled by the quadratic expression

$$P = 100(5 + t - 0.25t^2)$$

What was the rate of change of the population after 1, 2 and 3 years? What was the maximum population of the estate? What happened to the estate?

3.4 Graphical optimisation

Calculus has been described as the most powerful and useful invention of mathematics. Applications of calculus range over many areas of mathematics, physical science, engineering and the social sciences. This chapter has concentrated upon just one type of application – optimisation.

> Calculus can be used to find the local maximum and minimum values of a quantity. The quantity must first be expressed in terms of another simpler variable. You can then consider the graph of the relationship between the two variable quantities and, in particular, its stationary points.

When tackling real problems, the expressions obtained may be difficult to optimise algebraically. In such cases you can use a graph plotter to observe the overall shape of the curve and hence obtain from the graph the approximate positions of any local maxima and minima.

In question 3 of exercise 3 you should have obtained proportions for the guttering of

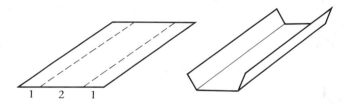

Gutters can have splayed sides:

Do class

> Intuitively, do you think that the amount of water which the gutter is able to carry can be increased by splaying its sides?
>
> Find an expression for the cross-sectional area of the splay-sided gutter in terms of some chosen variable quantity. Use a graph plotter to check if your intuition was correct.

TASKSHEET 4 — Box problems (page 47)   * Why calculus?

Sometimes, solving optimisation problems can be difficult algebraically. However, approximate answers can be obtained using a graph plotter.

TASKSHEET 5E — Optimisation problems (page 48) (OMIT)

Optimisation Problems

* Can be done on graphic calculator unless method is specified

REVIEW sheet $\frac{dy}{dx}$ (not $\frac{dx}{dy}$) Q1.

After working through this chapter you should:

1 be able to recognise and interpret rates of change in various contexts;

2 be able to use the derived function as an aid in graph-sketching;

3 be able to sketch quadratics and cubics rapidly;

4 be able to use sketches as an aid in optimisation problems;

5 be able to use the derived function as an aid in optimisation problems.

Omit Q6 of Review Sheet C

(6E)

SET REVISION SHEET FOR 1-3

Graph sketching

1 Make a copy of this sketch graph and indicate on it:

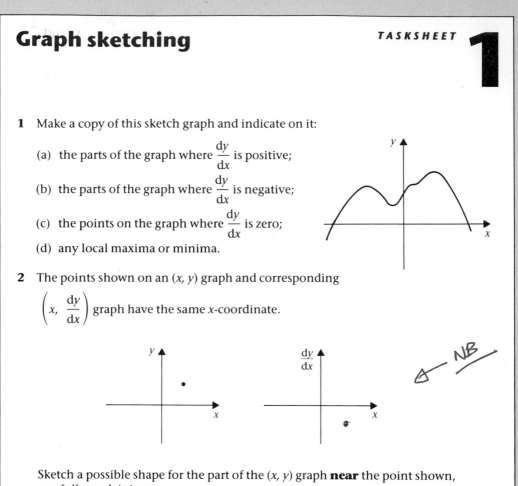

   (a) the parts of the graph where $\dfrac{dy}{dx}$ is positive;

   (b) the parts of the graph where $\dfrac{dy}{dx}$ is negative;

   (c) the points on the graph where $\dfrac{dy}{dx}$ is zero;

   (d) any local maxima or minima.

2 The points shown on an (x, y) graph and corresponding $\left(x, \dfrac{dy}{dx}\right)$ graph have the same x-coordinate.

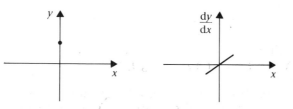

Sketch a possible shape for the part of the (x, y) graph **near** the point shown, carefully explaining your answer.

3 One point of an (x, y) graph and a segment of the corresponding $\left(x, \dfrac{dy}{dx}\right)$ graph are shown.

Sketch the (x, y) graph **near** $x = 0$, carefully explaining your answer.

4 Write a brief summary of what it means to say that a point on a graph is a local maximum or minimum and how you can determine from the gradient function whether the point is a local maximum or minimum.

Stationary points

1 For large x, the graph of $y = x^3 - 12x + 2$ is roughly the same shape as that of $y = x^3$.

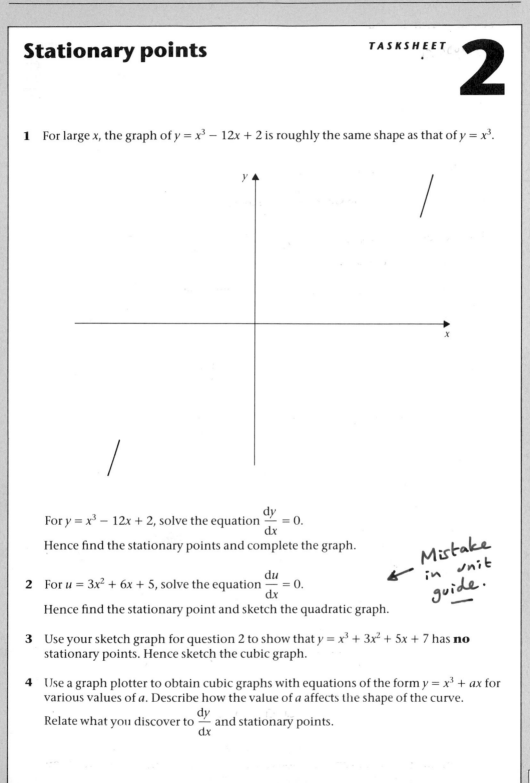

For $y = x^3 - 12x + 2$, solve the equation $\dfrac{dy}{dx} = 0$.

Hence find the stationary points and complete the graph.

Mistake in unit guide.

2 For $u = 3x^2 + 6x + 5$, solve the equation $\dfrac{du}{dx} = 0$.

Hence find the stationary point and sketch the quadratic graph.

3 Use your sketch graph for question 2 to show that $y = x^3 + 3x^2 + 5x + 7$ has **no** stationary points. Hence sketch the cubic graph.

4 Use a graph plotter to obtain cubic graphs with equations of the form $y = x^3 + ax$ for various values of a. Describe how the value of a affects the shape of the curve.

Relate what you discover to $\dfrac{dy}{dx}$ and stationary points.

Using stationary points

1 The population density (number of residents per unit area) of many cities depends roughly on the distance from the city centre.

For a particular city, the population density P in thousands of people per square kilometre at a distance r kilometres from the centre is given approximately by

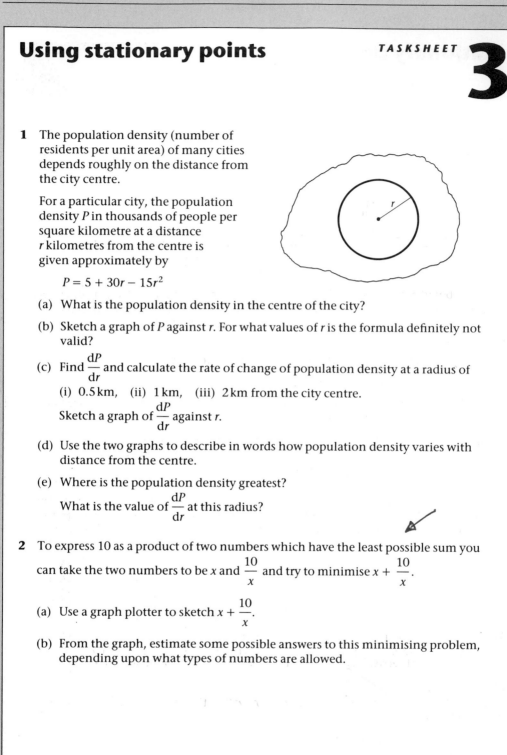

$$P = 5 + 30r - 15r^2$$

(a) What is the population density in the centre of the city?

(b) Sketch a graph of P against r. For what values of r is the formula definitely not valid?

(c) Find $\dfrac{\mathrm{d}P}{\mathrm{d}r}$ and calculate the rate of change of population density at a radius of

  (i) 0.5 km, (ii) 1 km, (iii) 2 km from the city centre.

  Sketch a graph of $\dfrac{\mathrm{d}P}{\mathrm{d}r}$ against r.

(d) Use the two graphs to describe in words how population density varies with distance from the centre.

(e) Where is the population density greatest?
  What is the value of $\dfrac{\mathrm{d}P}{\mathrm{d}r}$ at this radius?

2 To express 10 as a product of two numbers which have the least possible sum you can take the two numbers to be x and $\dfrac{10}{x}$ and try to minimise $x + \dfrac{10}{x}$.

(a) Use a graph plotter to sketch $x + \dfrac{10}{x}$.

(b) From the graph, estimate some possible answers to this minimising problem, depending upon what types of numbers are allowed.

Box problems

1

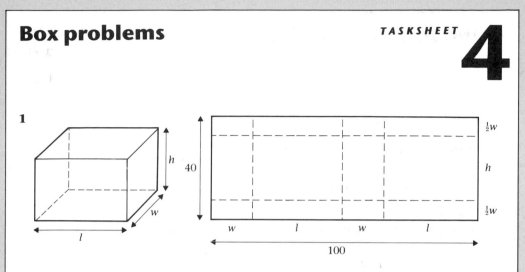

A cardboard box is to be made from a rectangular piece of card, 100 cm by 40 cm, by cutting and folding as necessary along the dashed lines shown in the right-hand diagram. The problem is to find the values of l, w and h which maximise the volume, V cm^3.

(a) Explain why $2l + 2w = 100$. Hence express l in terms of w.

(b) Similarly, find h in terms of w.

(c) The volume of the box is given by $V = whl$. Use your answers to (a) and (b) to show that $V = w(40 - w)(50 - w)$.

(d) Plot the graph of V against w. Hence find approximately the value of w corresponding to the maximum possible volume. What approximate dimensions will the box then have?

2 Small open-topped boxes are to be made out of sheet steel. Each box is to be made from a 6 cm by 4 cm rectangular piece of steel. A square will be cut from each corner, as shown in the diagram, and the remainder made into the box by bending along the dashed lines and welding.

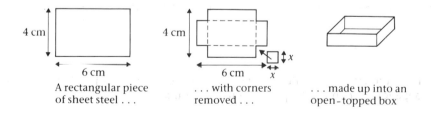

A rectangular piece of sheet steel . . .

. . . with corners removed . . .

. . . made up into an open-topped box

(a) If the squares cut out have side x cm, show that the volume of the box is V cm^3, where

$$V = x(4 - 2x)(6 - 2x)$$

(b) What should be the approximate dimensions if the volume of the box is to be as large as possible?

Optimisation problems

1 A mathematical ornament consists of a cone inside a sphere of radius 5 cm, such that the top and the perimeter of the base of the cone touch the sphere. Design the ornament so that the cone has maximum volume.

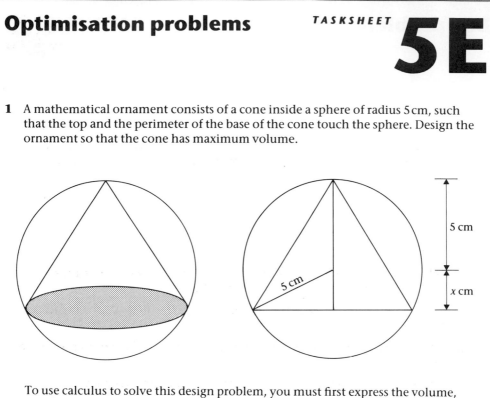

To use calculus to solve this design problem, you must first express the volume, V cm^3, of the cone in terms of another quantity which can then be varied to maximise V. The depth of the base of the cone below the centre of the sphere, x cm, seems a suitable quantity for this purpose.

(a) Why can x be neither greater than 5 nor less than -5?

(b) Without doing any calculations, write down what you think happens to the volume of the cone as x gradually changes from -5 to 5.

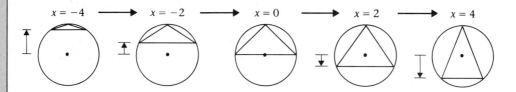

(c) Draw a rough sketch of the (x, V) graph which more or less fits your answer to part (b). Mark the value of x which you think will result in the greatest volume.

(d) The volume of a cone is $\frac{1}{3}\pi r^2 h$ where h is the height of the cone and r is the radius of its base. Calculate the volume of the cone for the value of x which you think gives the greatest volume.

(e) Suppose you choose as your variable not x, but y, where y cm is the height of the base of the cone above the lowest point of the sphere as shown in the diagram.

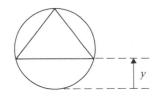

Again without doing any calculations, sketch what you think the graph (y, V) will look like.

(f) Whether you choose x or y is unimportant, except that the mathematics involved may be easier for one rather than the other.

Express V in terms of x, sketch the graph of V against x and use calculus to find the maximum value of V.

(g) Now express V in terms of y and again use calculus to find the maximum value of V.

Check that this results in exactly the same shape for the ornament.

(h) You could also have expressed V in terms of θ, where θ is the angle shown in the diagram.

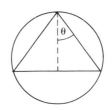

Without doing any calculations, sketch what you think the (θ, V) graph looks like.

Express V in terms of θ, use a graph plotter to plot the graph and determine the value of θ which maximises the volume. Check that this results in the same shape as before.

2 A bicycle manufacturer has designed a new model and has the problem of fixing the price in such a way that profits are maximised. After an initial cost of £50 000 to set up the production line it will cost £85 in labour, raw materials and components to produce each bike. Market research suggests that the firm can hope to sell 5000 bikes if the price is fixed at £100, but they can only expect to sell 1000 if the price is £200 per bike. They assume the relationship between price and demand is linear between these two extremes.

How many bikes would you advise the company to manufacture and at what price should they be sold?

4 Numerical integration

Programs for tap & mid-ord rule. (and to do by hand)

4.1 Areas under graphs

Suppose that water flows from a tap at a constant rate of 15 litres per minute.

This can be represented graphically.

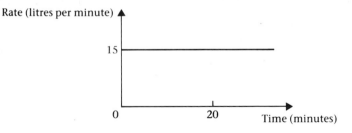

> What total volume of water flows from the tap in 20 minutes?
>
> How is this amount represented on the graph?

Areas under graphs can represent various quantities. The calculation of such areas is not always so simple.

TASKSHEET 1 — Areas (page 66)   *Add note to Q2*

Two of the possible methods for calculating areas under graphs will be developed in the next section. However, calculating an area is only part of the problem; knowing what quantity that area represents is also very important. You have probably met the idea of distance travelled being represented by the area under a (time, speed) graph, and in the example above, area represents a volume of water in litres.

The fact that the area represented litres could be deduced by considering the dimensions of the axes of the graph.

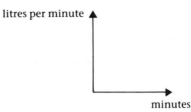

Area is calculated by multiplying a height by a width so, in the case above, the dimensions of area are

$$\frac{\text{litres}}{\text{minutes}} \times \text{minutes} = \text{litres}$$

Using the dimensions of the axes of a graph in this way is an essential step in solving many problems.

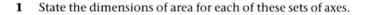

EXERCISE 1

1   State the dimensions of area for each of these sets of axes.

(a) km h^{-1} ... h

(b)   miles per litre ... litres

(c) cm^2 ... cm

(d) g cm^{-3} ... cm^3

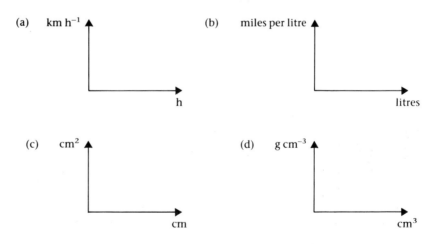

2   A graph shows how the speed of a turntable, recorded in revolutions per minute (r.p.m.), varies with time (seconds). What would one unit of area under such a graph represent?

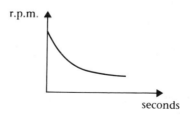

51

4.2 Estimating areas

Solving the problems on tasksheet 1 involved working out areas. The answers you obtained depended both upon the assumptions you made and on the method you used for estimating areas, for example, counting squares, dividing up into rectangles, triangles, etc.

Tasksheet 2 looks at two specific methods for estimating areas, both of which will be useful in later work.

TASKSHEET 2 – Methods of estimation (page 67)

Graph Paper needed

Take in

The diagrams below illustrate the mid-ordinate rule with three strips and the trapezium rule with two strips. It is customary when using either rule to keep all strip widths the same. This makes the calculation of the area much simpler.

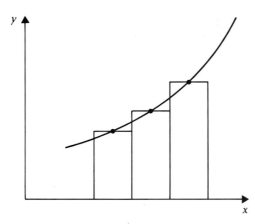

The mid-ordinate rule uses a series of rectangles to estimate the area under a graph. The height of each rectangle is determined by the height of the curve at the mid-point of the interval.

The trapezium rule uses a series of trapezia to estimate the area under a graph.

Underestimates or Over Estimates

EXAMPLE 1

A research firm has a circuit which is used to evaluate the performance of engines. A test car is fitted with a computer to record various information, and in one trial it is driven for 8 km round the circuit, gradually increasing in speed. The fuel consumption in $cm^3 \, km^{-1}$ is recorded at each kilometre.

Distance driven (km)	0	1	2	3	4	5	6	7	8
Fuel consumption ($cm^3 \, km^{-1}$)	95	70	62	57	55	60	72	87	109

(a) Sketch the graph, explain briefly the characteristics of the graph and state what the area under the graph represents.

(b) Calculate the area under the graph using

    (i) the mid-ordinate rule with four strips,
    (ii) the trapezium rule with four strips.

why not use these values + ½ bar at each end.

SOLUTION

(a)

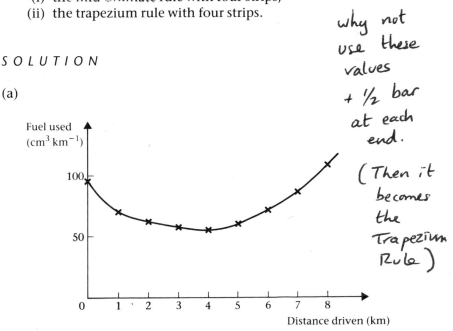

(Then it becomes the Trapezium Rule)

At low speed and at high speed the engine is less economical. As the speed increases from the start the fuel consumption, in $cm^3 \, km^{-1}$, decreases until the most economical speed is reached (after about 4 km); then the fuel consumption increases again.

The area represents the volume of fuel, in cm^3, used during the 8 km circuit.

(b) (i) **Mid-ordinate rule**

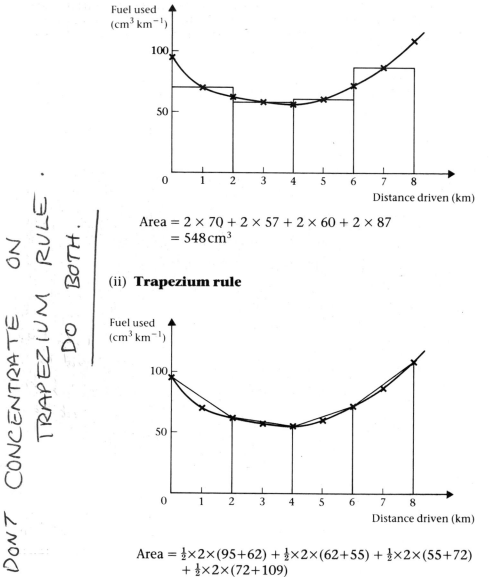

Area = $2 \times 70 + 2 \times 57 + 2 \times 60 + 2 \times 87$
     = $548 \, \text{cm}^3$

(ii) **Trapezium rule**

Area = $\frac{1}{2} \times 2 \times (95+62) + \frac{1}{2} \times 2 \times (62+55) + \frac{1}{2} \times 2 \times (55+72)$
     $+ \frac{1}{2} \times 2 \times (72+109)$
     = $582 \, \text{cm}^3$

Here the trapezium rule clearly over-estimates the area while the mid-ordinate rule under-estimates the area. The actual amount of fuel used is somewhere between the two values calculated.

> You could have estimated the amount of fuel used more accurately by using the trapezium rule with eight strips. Would this have over- or under-estimated the actual area?

DON'T CONCENTRATE ON TRAPEZIUM RULE. DO BOTH.

EXERCISE 2

1   A train is travelling at $20\,\mathrm{m\,s^{-1}}$ when the brakes are applied; t seconds later the speed of the train is given by $20 - 0.2t^2\,\mathrm{m\,s^{-1}}$. Sketch the (time, speed) graph and use the trapezium rule, with two-second intervals, to estimate the distance travelled by the train before it comes to rest.

2   A geologist does a survey of stalactites and stalagmites in a cave. In order to estimate their volumes, she measures their circumferences at different points along their lengths.

   Her measurements for one particular stalagmite are shown in the table below.

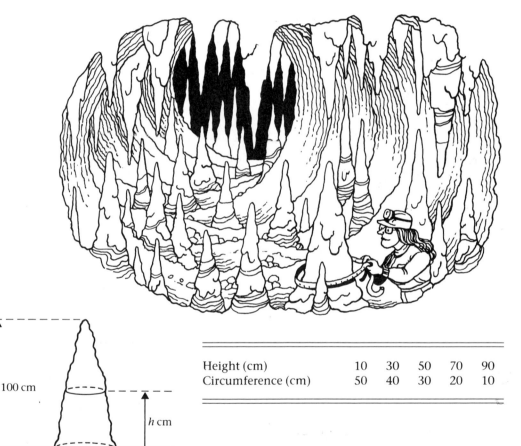

Height (cm)	10	30	50	70	90
Circumference (cm)	50	40	30	20	10

   (a)   Estimate the cross-sectional area of the stalagmite at each height and draw a graph which shows how the cross-sectional area changes with the height of the stalagmite. What assumptions have you made?

   (b)   Use the mid-ordinate rule to estimate the area under the graph. What does this area represent?

4.3 Integration

You have already seen that to solve some problems it is necessary to find areas under curves.

The **precise** value of the area under an (x, y) graph from $x = a$ to $x = b$ is denoted by

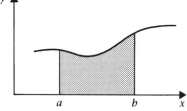

$$\int_a^b y\, dx$$

This notation may look complicated but it is very useful. It was introduced by Leibnitz in 1684 and is one of the reasons why Leibnitz's version of the calculus was more popular than Newton's.

The expression '$y\, dx$' denotes the area of a rectangle of height y and width dx.

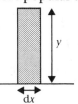

The symbol $\int$ is an old-fashioned form of the letter 's' and indicates that Leibnitz thought of the area under a curve as being

obtained by $\int$umming areas of lots of very thin rectangles.

The area under the graph of $y = x^2 + 4$ is shown in the diagram. The **precise** value of this area is written as

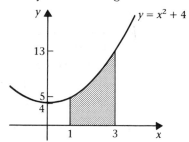

$$\int_1^3 (x^2 + 4)\, dx$$

The process of finding the area under a graph is called **integration** because it is, in essence, a process of combining many small parts to form a whole.

With reservations

The symbol $\int_a^b f(x)\, dx$ denotes the **precise** value of the area

underneath the graph of $y = f(x)$, between $x = a$ and $x = b$.

It is known as the **integral** of y with respect to x over the interval from a to b.

The integral can be found **approximately** by various numerical methods.

Consider the function $y = \sqrt{(4 - x^2)}$.

(a) Draw a diagram to illustrate the area represented by

$$\int_0^2 \sqrt{(4 - x^2)}\, dx$$

← from area of circle/4

(b) What is the precise value of this integral?

(c) Use the mid-ordinate rule with two strips to estimate this integral.

Do?.

EXERCISE 3

1 Draw the graph of $y = x$ and indicate the area represented by the integral

$$\int_0^3 x\, dx.$$ Find the precise value of this integral.

2 Calculate: (a) $\displaystyle\int_1^4 x\, dx$ (b) $\displaystyle\int_1^3 5\, dx$ (c) $\displaystyle\int_1^4 (2x + 3)\, dx$

3 To estimate, for example, the depth of a well or the height of a cliff, you can use the fact that the downward speed of a dropped stone increases by approximately $10\,\mathrm{m\,s^{-1}}$ each second.

From the top of a particular cliff, a stone takes 5 seconds to reach the sea.

(a) Find the speed of the stone t seconds after being dropped.

(b) Express the height of the cliff as an integral.

(c) Find the height of the clif.

4

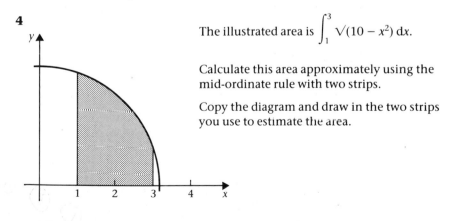

The illustrated area is $\displaystyle\int_1^3 \sqrt{(10 - x^2)}\, dx$.

Calculate this area approximately using the mid-ordinate rule with two strips.

Copy the diagram and draw in the two strips you use to estimate the area.

4.4 Numerical methods

In the previous section you obtained an approximation for π using the mid-ordinate rule with just two strips. You can improve your estimate by using more (thinner) strips.

The diagram shows the area represented by

$$\int_0^2 \sqrt{(4 - x^2)} \, dx$$

divided into 10 strips. (Only a few of the strips are shown.)

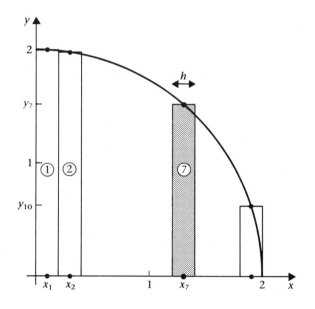

What are the values of:

(a) the width, h, of each strip;

(b) x_1, y_1, x_2, y_2;

(c) the areas of strips ① and ②;

(d) x_7, y_7 and the area of strip ⑦ ?

To obtain an accurate estimate of an area you need to perform a large number of calculations. It is therefore convenient to use a calculator or microcomputer, as on tasksheet 3.

TASKSHEET 3 — To the limit (page 69)

The trapezium and the mid-ordinate rules with n strips both involve the sum of n areas.

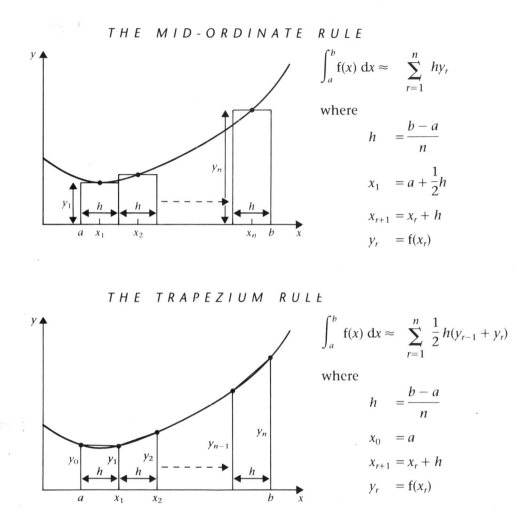

THE MID-ORDINATE RULE

$$\int_a^b f(x)\, dx \approx \sum_{r=1}^{n} hy_r$$

where

$$h = \frac{b-a}{n}$$

$$x_1 = a + \frac{1}{2}h$$

$$x_{r+1} = x_r + h$$

$$y_r = f(x_r)$$

THE TRAPEZIUM RULE

$$\int_a^b f(x)\, dx \approx \sum_{r=1}^{n} \frac{1}{2}h(y_{r-1} + y_r)$$

where

$$h = \frac{b-a}{n}$$

$$x_0 = a$$

$$x_{r+1} = x_r + h$$

$$y_r = f(x_r)$$

The two rules can be summarised as follows

The mid-ordinate rule

$$\int_a^b y\, dx \approx hy_1 + hy_2 + hy_3 + \ldots + hy_n$$

The trapezium rule

$$\int_a^b y\, dx \approx \frac{1}{2}h(y_0 + y_1) + \frac{1}{2}h(y_1 + y_2) + \ldots + \frac{1}{2}h(y_{n-1} + y_n)$$

$$\approx \frac{h}{2}\left[\,\text{Ends} + 2\,(\text{Middles})\,\right]$$

As you take more and more strips, the effect near the mid-point of any strip is similar to the effect you observe when a microcomputer is used to zoom in on a small part of a graph.

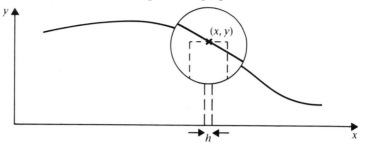

The area estimate given by either the trapezium or the mid-ordinate rule will become closer and closer to the true value, at least for all locally straight graphs.

For the graph of $y = \sqrt{(4 - x^2)}$ you will have noticed that the trapezium rule consistently under-estimates the true area whereas the mid-ordinate rule always over-estimates it.

The trapezium rule approximates a graph with a series of chords and it is easy to tell whether it will over- or under-estimate the area.

Over-estimate   Under-estimate

To predict if the mid-ordinate rule will over- or under-estimate an area, it is helpful to think of it as producing trapezia rather than rectangles!

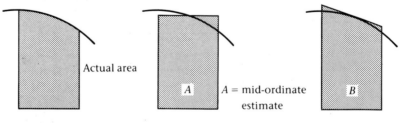

Actual area

A A = mid-ordinate B

estimate

Explain why the area of trapezium B is precisely the same as the area of rectangle A.

Thus, you can think of the mid-ordinate rule as approximating a graph with a series of tangents to the graph.

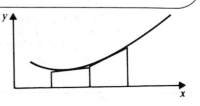

EXERCISE 4

1 State, where it is clear, whether a mid-ordinate rule estimate of each of the following areas will be too large or too small.

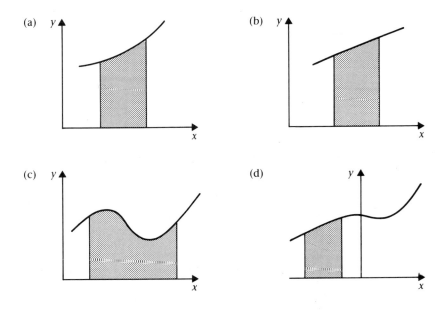

(a)   (b)

(c)   (d)

2 Repeat question 1 for the trapezium rule.

3 Among other things, a firm manufactures two types of metal alloy casting which will be machined into components for use in the car industry. The castings are in the form of prisms whose cross-sectional areas are shown below. (Measurements are in cm.)

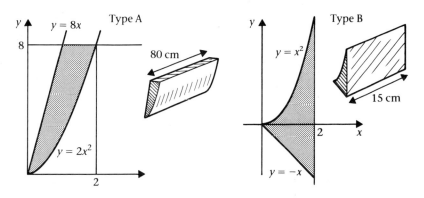

The firm receives an order for 12 000 castings of type A and 8000 of type B. The production manager needs to calculate how much alloy to prepare. He does this by calculating the combined volume of all the castings and then adding on 5% for wastage. Calculate this volume and give your answer in cubic metres.

4.5 'Negative' areas

As in the following example, areas below the *x*-axis often have a special significance.

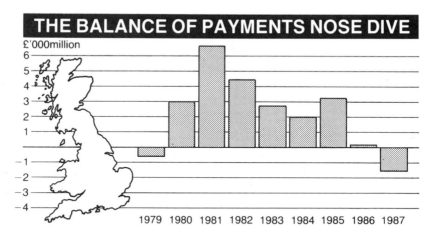

THE BALANCE OF PAYMENTS NOSE DIVE

£'000million

1979 1980 1981 1982 1983 1984 1985 1986 1987

(a) Use the data represented above to estimate the total trade balance from 1979 to 1987.

(b) Using a numerical method, evaluate the integral

$$\int_a^b (3x^2 - 18x + 24)\,\mathrm{d}x$$

for intervals given by

$a = 1, b = 2; \quad a = 2, b = 4; \quad a = 1, b = 4.$

Comment on the calculations above with reference to the graph given below.

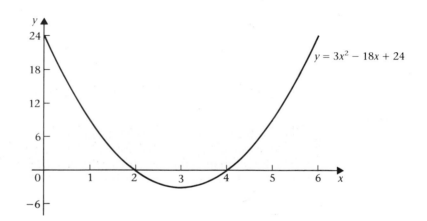

$y = 3x^2 - 18x + 24$

The mid-ordinate rule assigns positive values to areas above the x-axis and negative values to areas below the x-axis. This is because it uses sums of terms, each of the form yh.

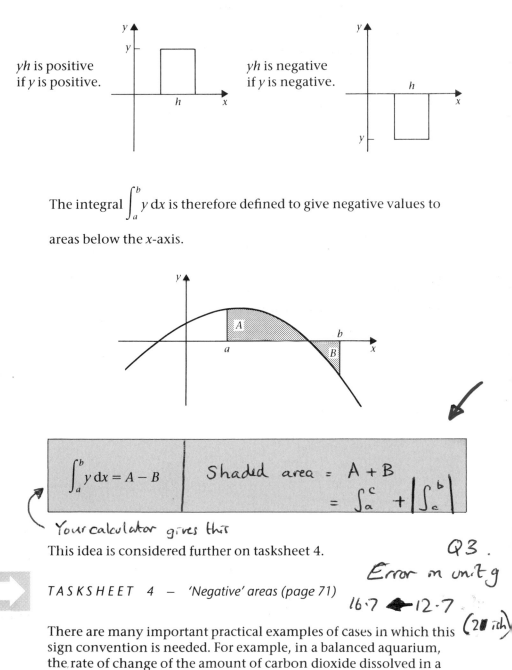

yh is positive if y is positive.

yh is negative if y is negative.

The integral $\int_a^b y\,dx$ is therefore defined to give negative values to areas below the x-axis.

$$\int_a^b y\,dx = A - B$$

Shaded area $= A + B$

$$= \int_a^c + \left| \int_c^b \right|$$

Your calculator gives this

This idea is considered further on tasksheet 4.

TASKSHEET 4 — 'Negative' areas (page 71)

Q3.
Error in unit g
16·7 ← 12·7
(20 ish)

There are many important practical examples of cases in which this sign convention is needed. For example, in a balanced aquarium, the rate of change of the amount of carbon dioxide dissolved in a litre of water is found to have the following daily pattern:

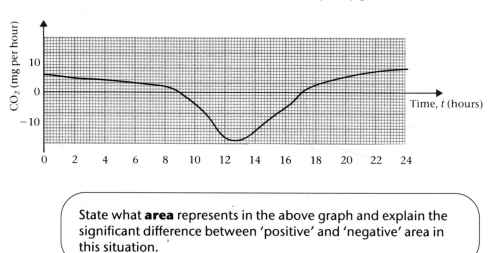

State what **area** represents in the above graph and explain the significant difference between 'positive' and 'negative' area in this situation.

EXERCISE 5

1 Use the graph for the balanced aquarium to answer the following questions.

(a) During what part of the day is the amount of carbon dioxide dissolved in the aquarium water increasing? Estimate the total increase during this part of the day.

(b) Estimate the increase in the amount of carbon dioxide dissolved during a full 24-hour cycle.

2 (a) Sketch the graph of $y = x^2 - x - 2$.

(b) Estimate

(i) $\int_{-4}^{4} y \, dx$ (ii) $\int_{-4}^{-1} y \, dx$ (iii) $\int_{-1}^{2} y \, dx$ (iv) $\int_{2}^{4} y \, dx$

(c) Estimate the area enclosed between the graph and the x-axis.

3 Water flows both into and out of a tank. The flow out is at a constant rate of 3 litres per minute, whereas the flow in starts off at 15 litres per minute but then decreases with time. The supervising engineer decides that the flow in at time t minutes may be modelled by

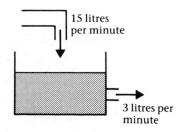

$\dfrac{15}{t^2 + 1}$ litres per minute.

The tank initially contains 50 litres of water.

(a) The net flow into the tank is given by the expression

$$\frac{15}{t^2 + 1} - 3$$

Use a graph plotter to show the graph of this (time, flow) function. Why is $t = 2$ an important point on the graph?

(b) What does area under the (time, flow) graph represent and what is the significant difference between 'positive' and 'negative' areas?

(c) Estimate

$$\int \left(\frac{15}{t^2 + 1} - 3 \right) dt$$

over the time intervals

(i) $t = 0$ to $t = 2$ (ii) $t = 2$ to $t = 5$ (iii) $t = 0$ to $t = 5$.

Explain the meaning of your answer in each case.

(d) How much water is there in the tank after 2 minutes and after 5 minutes? About how long will it take to empty the tank completely?

TASKSHEET 5E — Traffic (page 72)

After working through this chapter you should:

1 be able to recognise what the area under a graph represents;

2 understand the process of estimating areas under graphs using the mid-ordinate rule;

3 understand the process of estimating areas under graphs using the trapezium rule;

4 understand the notation

$$\int_a^b y \, dx$$

can be negative

Poor

used to denote the **precise** area under a graph;

5 understand why increasing the number of strips increases the accuracy of the mid-ordinate and the trapezium rules;

6 understand how to use a numerical method to estimate areas;

7 understand why areas below the x-axis are calculated as being negative and areas above the x-axis are positive.

65

Areas

1

Over a 20-minute period, the rate of flow from the oil tank is recorded at two-minute intervals.

Time (minutes)	1	3	5	7	9	11	13	15	17	19
Rate of flow (litres per minute)	46.3	39.7	34.0	29.2	25.0	21.4	18.4	15.8	13.5	11.6

(a) Estimate the volume drained from the tank during this 20-minute period.

(b) What assumptions have you made?

(c) Explain your method using a (time, rate of flow) graph.

2

Depth readings are taken across a river of width 18 metres. Depths at various distances from the left bank are shown in the table.

Distance (m)	0	2	4	6	8	10	12	14	16	18
Depth (m)	0	0.2	1	2	3.1	3.8	3.8	3.9	3.5	0

Describe a method of estimating the cross-sectional area of the river from these figures. *and work out.*

Methods of estimation

TASKSHEET **2**

Graph Paper Needed.

Worth taking in.

1

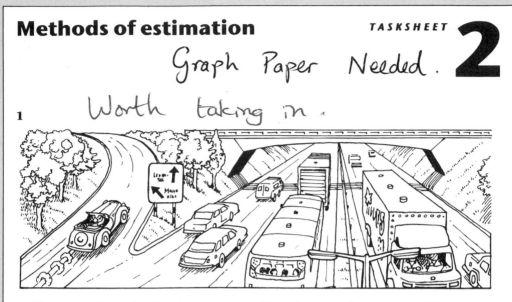

The driver of a car leaving the motorway allows the car to decrease in speed gradually over a 60-second time period. The speed is recorded at 10-second intervals to give the table below.

Time (s)	5	15	25	35	45	55
Speed (m s^{-1})	29.9	23.1	19.2	17.0	15.7	15.0

(a) Plot the (time, speed) coordinates from the table on graph paper and draw the graph for times ranging from 0 to 60 seconds. What does the area under the graph represent?

You need to use the information in the table to estimate the distance the car travels during the 60 seconds. Although common sense may tell you that the speed of the car is continuously changing with time, you can approximate the motion in the following way. Suppose the car travels at a constant $29.9 \, \text{m s}^{-1}$ during the time interval $0 \to 10$ seconds, then instantly changes speed and travels at $23.1 \, \text{m s}^{-1}$ during the time interval $10 \to 20$ seconds, etc. (call this the 'constant speed' model).

(b) Use this model to estimate the distance the car travels during the 60 seconds.

(c) Superimpose the 'constant speed' model graph on the graph you drew for (a).

(d) Shade in the area of the graph which corresponds to your answer to (b) and, by considering this area, explain why your answer is a good estimate of the actual distance travelled.

(e) Do you think your answer to (b) over-estimates or under-estimates the actual distance travelled? Explain why.

The method of estimation used above is called the **mid-ordinate rule**.

2 Suppose readings of the speed of the car were taken at different times.

Time (s)	0	10	20	30	40	50	60
Speed (m s^{-1})	35.0	26.0	20.9	18.0	16.3	15.3	14.7

(a) Draw the (time, speed) graph for times ranging from 0 to 60 seconds.

Although the graph is obviously curved, you can approximate it with a series of six straight line segments by joining the known points on the graph. In this model of the car's motion you assume that the car's speed decreases uniformly during each 10-second interval.

(b) Superimpose this model as a graph on the (time, speed) graph you have just drawn.

(c) Use the model to estimate the distance travelled by the car during the 60 seconds.

(d) Does the method over-estimate or under-estimate the actual distance travelled?

This second method of estimation is called the **trapezium rule.**

To the limit

TASKSHEET

3

THE MID-ORDINATE RULE

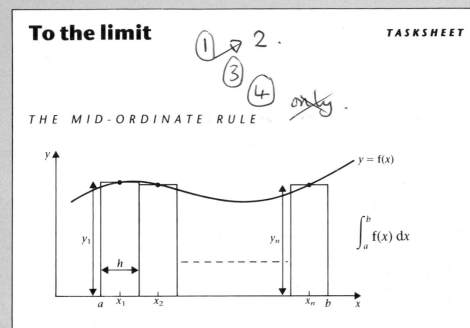

$$\int_a^b f(x)\,dx$$

Consider the area represented by the integral above to be split up into n strips of equal width, h.

Using the mid-ordinate rule to approximate the integral, the area of the first strip would be calculated as hy_1, the second strip would be hy_2, and so on.

1 (a) Express h in terms of a, b and n.

  (b) Express x_1 in terms of a and h.

  (c) By how much do you increase x each time you move up a strip?

To get a very accurate estimate of the integral you might have to use a very large number of strips. Making a large number of routine calculations is a task well-suited to a programmable calculator or computer. Help is given on technology datasheet: *Numerical integration*.

2 $\displaystyle\int_0^2 \sqrt{(4 - x^2)}\,dx = \pi$

  (a) Use the mid-ordinate rule to evaluate the integral above with

   (i) 10 strips (ii) 20 strips (iii) 40 strips (iv) 80 strips

   and so on. Compare each of your estimates with an accurate value for π, and comment on how the error changes as you increase the number of strips.

  (b) Approximately how many strips do you need to estimate π to an accuracy of 4 decimal places?

69

THE TRAPEZIUM RULE

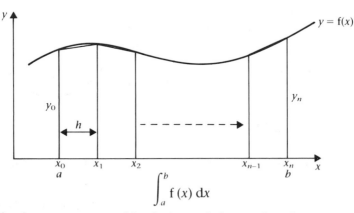

$$\int_a^b f(x)\, dx$$

Again consider the area represented by the integral above to be split up into n strips of equal width, h.

Using the trapezium rule, the area of the first strip would be $\frac{1}{2}h(y_0 + y_1)$, the area of the second strip would be $\frac{1}{2}h(y_1 + y_2)$, and so on.

3 Suppose you evaluate the integral $\int_0^2 \sqrt{(4 - x^2)}\, dx$ with 10 strips using the trapezium rule.

(a) What would be the area of the first strip?

(b) Explain carefully how you would work out the area of strip ⑦.

4 Repeat question 2 for the trapezium rule, using a programmable calculator or computer. (Help is given on technology datasheet: *Numerical integration*.)

'Negative' areas

1 (a) Evaluate (i) $\displaystyle\int_2^{13} (3x^2 - 30x + 48)\, \mathrm{d}x$

(ii) $\displaystyle\int_8^{10} (3x^2 - 30x + 48)\, \mathrm{d}x$

(iii) $\displaystyle\int_2^{10} (3x^2 - 30x + 48)\, \mathrm{d}x$

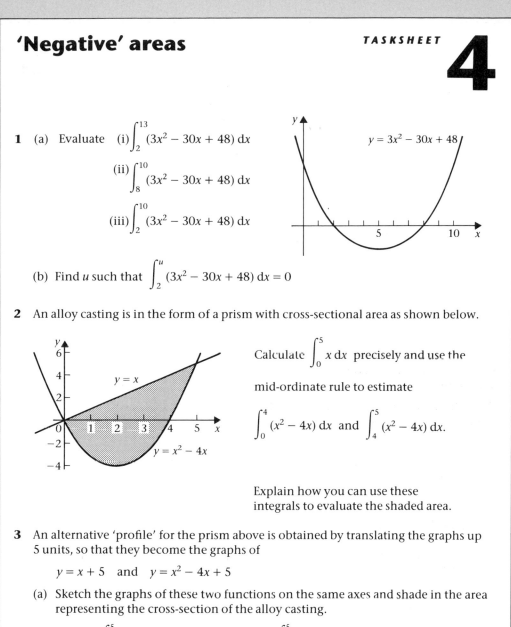

$y = 3x^2 - 30x + 48$

(b) Find u such that $\displaystyle\int_2^u (3x^2 - 30x + 48)\, \mathrm{d}x = 0$

2 An alloy casting is in the form of a prism with cross-sectional area as shown below.

$y = x$

$y = x^2 - 4x$

Calculate $\displaystyle\int_0^5 x\, \mathrm{d}x$ precisely and use the mid-ordinate rule to estimate

$$\int_0^4 (x^2 - 4x)\, \mathrm{d}x \quad \text{and} \quad \int_4^5 (x^2 - 4x)\, \mathrm{d}x.$$

Explain how you can use these integrals to evaluate the shaded area.

3 An alternative 'profile' for the prism above is obtained by translating the graphs up 5 units, so that they become the graphs of

$$y = x + 5 \quad \text{and} \quad y = x^2 - 4x + 5$$

(a) Sketch the graphs of these two functions on the same axes and shade in the area representing the cross-section of the alloy casting.

(b) Evaluate $\displaystyle\int_0^5 (x + 5)\, \mathrm{d}x$ precisely, estimate $\displaystyle\int_0^5 (x^2 - 4x + 5)\, \mathrm{d}x$ and use your answers to calculate the shaded area, confirming your answer to question 2.

Traffic

5E

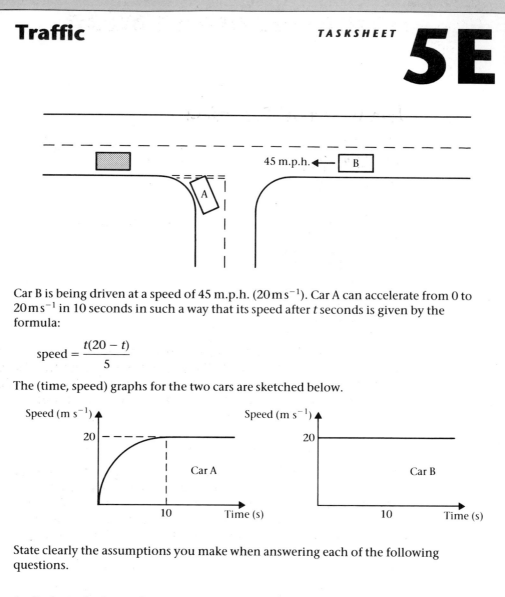

Car B is being driven at a speed of 45 m.p.h. ($20\,\mathrm{m\,s}^{-1}$). Car A can accelerate from 0 to $20\,\mathrm{m\,s}^{-1}$ in 10 seconds in such a way that its speed after t seconds is given by the formula:

$$\text{speed} = \frac{t(20 - t)}{5}$$

The (time, speed) graphs for the two cars are sketched below.

State clearly the assumptions you make when answering each of the following questions.

1 Evaluate the integral

$$\int_0^{10} \frac{t(20 - t)}{5}\, dt$$

and explain what information it gives you about the motion of car A.

2 What is the least distance B can be from A at the start of the manoeuvre if B is to avoid slowing down?

3 If 1200 cars per hour use the road, is A likely to find a gap of sufficient length?

5 Algebraic integration

5.1 The integral function

In chapter 4, you used the mid-ordinate rule with two strips to obtain the approximation to the area under the graph of $y = \sqrt{(4 - x^2)}$ given below.

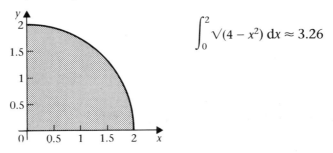

$$\int_0^2 \sqrt{(4 - x^2)} \, dx \approx 3.26$$

This is a value for the area of a quarter of a circle of radius 2 units, which you could use to estimate the area of the whole circle. Whilst this is one way of finding the area of the circle, it is unlikely to be the way you would choose because you already know the formula

$$A = \pi r^2$$

for the area of a circle of radius r units.

The formula $A = \pi r^2$ for the area of a circle was known in classical times. In the seventeenth century, the calculus developed by Leibnitz and Newton enabled formulas to be obtained for various areas. Today, calculators and computers can be used to work out such areas by numerical methods but there are still advantages in possessing simple formulas. This section will look at formulas for the areas under the graphs of a few simple functions, starting with $f(x) = x$.

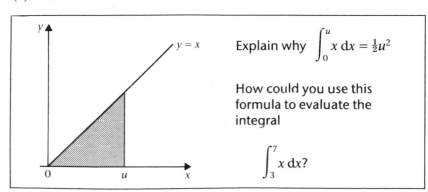

Explain why $\displaystyle\int_0^u x \, dx = \tfrac{1}{2}u^2$

How could you use this formula to evaluate the integral

$$\int_3^7 x \, dx?$$

TASKSHEET 1 — *Finding integral functions (page 87)*

For areas measured from $x = 0$ you have found that

$$f(x) = x \quad \Rightarrow \quad A(x) = \tfrac{1}{2}x^2$$

and you have some numerical evidence for the result that

$$f(x) = x^2 \quad \Rightarrow \quad A(x) = \tfrac{1}{3}x^3$$

You can now use these area functions, called **integral functions**, to evaluate integrals precisely and easily.

E X A M P L E   1

Sketch the graph of $y = x^2$. Calculate the area given by

$$\int_{2.5}^{4} x^2 \, dx$$

S O L U T I O N

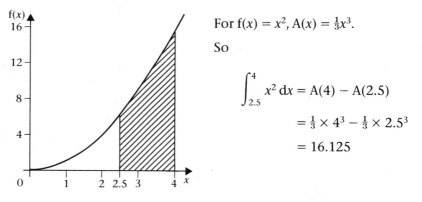

For $f(x) = x^2$, $A(x) = \tfrac{1}{3}x^3$.

So

$$\int_{2.5}^{4} x^2 \, dx = A(4) - A(2.5)$$

$$= \tfrac{1}{3} \times 4^3 - \tfrac{1}{3} \times 2.5^3$$

$$= 16.125$$

A special notation is used when writing out the evaluation of integrals. For example,

$$\int_{2.5}^{4} x^2 \, dx = \left[\tfrac{1}{3}x^3 \right]_{2.5}^{4}$$

where the new notation on the right-hand side shows the integral function, $\tfrac{1}{3}x^3$, and also shows the limits, 2.5 and 4. The full solution to example 1 would therefore be written:

$$\int_{2.5}^{4} x^2 \, dx = \left[\tfrac{1}{3}x^3 \right]_{2.5}^{4} = \tfrac{1}{3} \times 4^3 - \tfrac{1}{3} \times 2.5^3 = 16.125$$

> Using this new notation, evaluate $\displaystyle\int_2^5 x^2\,dx$.
>
> On a sketch of $y = x^2$, shade the area you have found.

EXAMPLE 2

An object starts from rest and its speed $v\,\text{m\,s}^{-1}$ at time t seconds is given by $v = t^2$. Calculate the distance travelled in the third second of its motion.

SOLUTION

The (time, speed) graph shows that the distance travelled in the third second, as represented by the shaded area, will be given by

$$\int_2^3 t^2\,dt = \left[\tfrac{1}{3}t^3\right]_2^3$$

$$= \tfrac{27}{3} - \tfrac{8}{3}$$

$$= \tfrac{19}{3}$$

The distance travelled is $6\tfrac{1}{3}$ m.

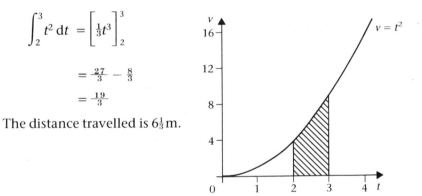

EXERCISE 1

1 (a) Sketch the graph of $y = x^2$.

(b) Use the symmetry of the quadratic graph in part (a) to explain why

$$\int_2^4 x^2\,dx = \int_{-4}^{-2} x^2\,dx$$

(c) Use the formula for the integral function to confirm algebraically that

$$\int_2^4 x^2\,dx = \int_{-4}^{-2} x^2\,dx$$

2 (a) Using the integral function, evaluate algebraically

(i) $\displaystyle\int_{-3}^{-1.5} x^2\,dx$ (ii) $\displaystyle\int_{-1.5}^{1.5} x^2\,dx$ (iii) $\displaystyle\int_{1.5}^{3} x^2\,dx$ (iv) $\displaystyle\int_{-1.5}^{3} x^2\,dx$

(b) Write down any relationships which connect two or more of these integrals. Explain, with the aid of a sketch graph, why these relationships are true.

3 (a)

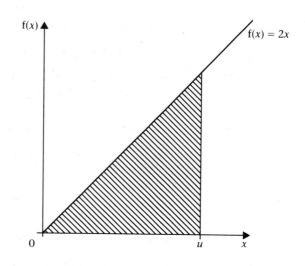

Calculate the shaded area in terms of u.

(b) What is the formula for the integral function?

4 For the function $f(v) = 3v$,

(a) sketch and shade the area between the graph and the horizontal axis, between the limits $v = 0$ and $v = u$;

(b) calculate the shaded area in terms of u.

5 Repeat question 4 using the following functions.

(a) $f(x) = 2$ (b) $g(t) = -3$

(c) $f(t) = 2t$ (d) $g(v) = -3v$

6 Write down the integral function for

(a) $f(x) = m$ (b) $g(x) = mx$

when m is any constant and areas are measured from $x = 0$.

5.2 Polynomial integrals

So far, you have met the following integral functions:

(a) If $f(x) = m$, then $A(x) = mx$;

(b) If $f(x) = mx$, then $A(x) = \frac{1}{2}mx^2$;

(c) If $f(x) = x^2$, then $A(x) = \frac{1}{3}x^3$.

> What do you think the integral functions are for:
>
> (a) $f(x) = x^3$ (b) $f(x) = 2x^2$ (c) $f(x) = x^2 - 3x$?
>
> Check your conjectures using the 'area' option on a graph plotter. Guidance is given on technology datasheet: *Area functions*.

Further work on polynomial integrals is given on tasksheet 2. UNIT G.

TASKSHEET 2 — Polynomials (page 88)

Mīstake P39

You now have the following rule for integrating ② a) $\int 3\,dx$ b) $\int x^3\,dx$

> A polynomial function of the form $f(x) = a + bx + cx^2 + dx^3$
>
> has integral function $A(x) = ax + \frac{1}{2}bx^2 + \frac{1}{3}cx^3 + \frac{1}{4}dx^4$.

EXAMPLE 3

(a) Evaluate the integral $\displaystyle\int_0^3 (x-4)(x-2)(x+1)\,dx$.

(b) Use a suitable sketch to show the area calculated.

SOLUTION

(a) $\displaystyle\int_0^3 (x-4)(x-2)(x+1)\,dx = \int_0^3 (x^3 - 5x^2 + 2x + 8)\,dx$

$$= \left[\frac{x^4}{4} - \frac{5x^3}{3} + \frac{2x^2}{2} + 8x \right]_0^3 = 8.25$$

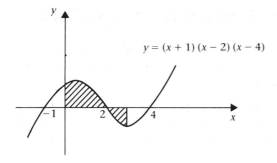

$y = (x + 1)(x - 2)(x - 4)$

(b) The integral is the sum of a positive part from $x = 0$ to $x = 2$ and a negative part from $x = 2$ to $x = 3$.

EXERCISE 2

1

(a) Write down the integral which represents the shaded area.

$y = 3x^2 - 5$

(b) Calculate this area.

error in back $\frac{1}{3} \to \frac{2}{3}$

2 (a) Evaluate $\displaystyle\int_{-2}^{1} (t^3 + 2t^2 - 3)\, dt$.

(b) Using a suitable sketch, explain why your answer is negative.

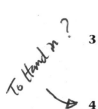

To Hand in ?

3 (a) Sketch the graph of $y = x^3 - 2x^2 - 5x + 6$, showing clearly where the curve cuts the x-axis.

(b) Calculate the total area enclosed by the curve and the x-axis.

4 A stone is projected vertically upwards such that its speed ($v\,\text{ms}^{-1}$) after t seconds is given by

$$v = 5(5 - 2t)$$

(a) How far does the stone travel in the first two seconds?

(b) After how many seconds does it reach its maximum height?

(c) Calculate the maximum height the stone will reach.

5.3 Numerical or algebraic integration?

Many problems of integration can be solved easily using an appropriate algorithm on a hand-held calculator. So why have a formula for integral functions?

If you just want a numerical answer then numerical integration is fine. But in this section you will see that <u>if you want to understand what is going on in a problem, then having a formula can be very helpful.</u>

EXAMPLE 4

A fruit farmer estimates that the average apple tree yields 45 kg of fruit and that it takes about 3 hours to pick all the apples. The fruit pickers are paid at a rate of £6 per hour and the farmer sells the apples for 60p per kg. Productivity decreases with time; in other words a person can pick more apples during the first half hour than during the last as the apples become harder to reach. The farmer assumes productivity decreases linearly with time.

DO

To give an area of 45

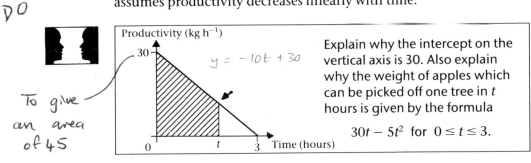

Productivity (kg h⁻¹)

$y = -10t + 30$

Explain why the intercept on the vertical axis is 30. Also explain why the weight of apples which can be picked off one tree in t hours is given by the formula

$$30t - 5t^2 \text{ for } 0 \le t \le 3.$$

If all the apples on a tree are picked, the farmer makes a profit of £9 (45 kg at 60p less 3 hours at £6). If, however, the person picking the apples stops after t hours, then the profit, £P, is obtained by calculating $(30t - 5t^2)$ kg at £0.60 less t hours at £6.

$$P = 0.6(30t - 5t^2) - 6t = 12t - 3t^2 \quad (0 \le t \le 3)$$

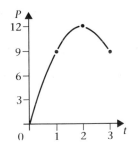

You can see that the farmer can increase the profit to £12 per tree by instructing the workers to spend only 2 hours on each tree and leave the last few apples for the birds.

Another example illustrating the advantages of having a formula is given on tasksheet 3.

TASKSHEET 3 — Catalyst renewal (page 89)

5.4 The fundamental theorem of calculus

You have been able to calculate some integrals precisely by first finding an integral function. For example, $x^3 + x$ is an integral function for $3x^2 + 1$ and so

$$\int_3^5 (3x^2 + 1)\, dx = \left[x^3 + x \right]_3^5$$

What simple relationship is there between a function and its integral function? The table below may help you to spot the connection.

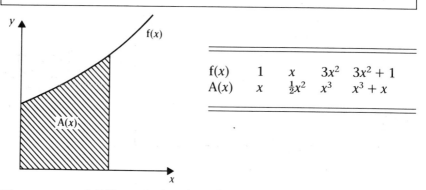

$f(x)$	1	x	$3x^2$	$3x^2 + 1$
$A(x)$	x	$\frac{1}{2}x^2$	x^3	$x^3 + x$

The process of differentiation (e.g. finding gradients) is an inverse process to that of integration (e.g. finding areas).

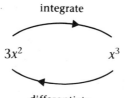

integrate

$3x^2 \qquad x^3$

differentiate

This remarkable relationship is called the **fundamental theorem of calculus.**

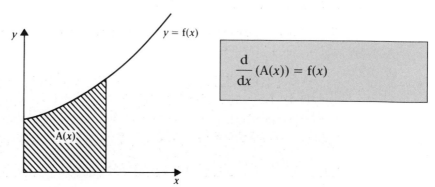

$$\frac{d}{dx}(A(x)) = f(x)$$

The graphs of all differentiable functions are locally straight, so it is sensible to investigate the connection between differentiation and integration by first considering linear functions.

TASKSHEET 4 — Straight line segments (page 91)

Dodgy
Do with them

You have seen that, for a graph made up of connected straight line segments,

$$\int_a^b g'(x)\,dx = g(b) - g(a)$$

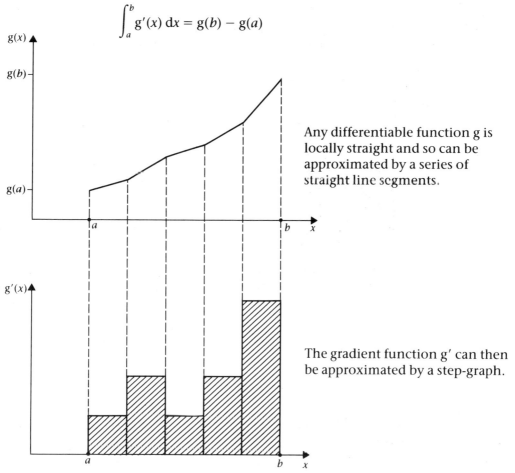

Any differentiable function g is locally straight and so can be approximated by a series of straight line segments.

The gradient function g′ can then be approximated by a step-graph.

This does not **prove** the fundamental theorem of calculus but at least indicates why:

For any differentiable function, f,

$$\int_a^b f'(x)\,dx = f(b) - f(a)$$

81

The fact that integration and differentiation are inverse operations should not come as a surprise when you think about the way in which (time, speed) and (time, distance) graphs are related. Given a (time, distance) function you differentiate to find speed and given a (time, speed) function you integrate to find distance.

The fundamental theorem gives a method of integrating which is easy to use. You must find a function which, when differentiated, gives the function you wish to integrate!

EXAMPLE 5

(a) Differentiate $\frac{1}{4}x^4 - x^3 - \frac{1}{2}x^2 + 3x + 1$.

(b) Hence find $\int_1^3 (x^3 - 3x^2 - x + 3)\,dx$.

SOLUTION

(a) $\dfrac{d}{dx}(\frac{1}{4}x^4 - x^3 - \frac{1}{2}x^2 + 3x + 1) = x^3 - 3x^2 - x + 3$

(b) $\int_1^3 (x^3 - 3x^2 - x + 3)\,dx = \left[\frac{1}{4}x^4 - x^3 - \frac{1}{2}x^2 + 3x + 1\right]_1^3$

$$= (-1\frac{1}{4}) - (2\frac{3}{4}) = -4$$

EXERCISE 3

1 (a) Evaluate

(i) $\int_{-1}^1 (x^3 - 3x^2 - x + 3)\,dx$ (ii) $\int_{-1}^3 (x^3 - 3x^2 - x + 3)\,dx$

(b) Sketch the graph of $y = x^3 - 3x^2 - x + 3$. Hence explain the connection between your answers to (a) and the value of $\int_1^3 (x^3 - 3x^2 - x + 3)\,dx$ obtained in the solution to example 5.

2 (a) Differentiate $x^3 - 5x^2 + 7$.   (b) Hence find $\int_1^2 (3x^2 - 10x)\,dx$.

3 (a) If $\int_c^d g(x)\,dx = \left[5x^2 + 3x\right]_c^d$, write down g(x).

(b) If $\int_a^b h(t)\,dt = \left[2t^3 - 7\right]_a^b$, write down h(t).

4 Some areas which cannot be calculated directly can be obtained by considering a combination of integrals.

(a)

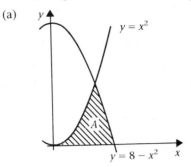

(i) Explain why the shaded area is given by

$$A = \int_0^a x^2 \, dx + \int_a^b (8 - x^2) \, dx$$

where a and b are to be found.

(ii) Find the shaded area A.

(b) Find the shaded areas.

(i)   (ii)   (iii)

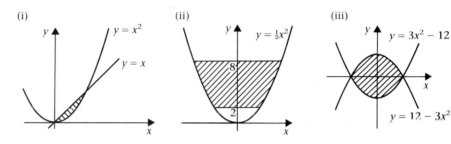

5 Find c if the shaded area is 6 square units.

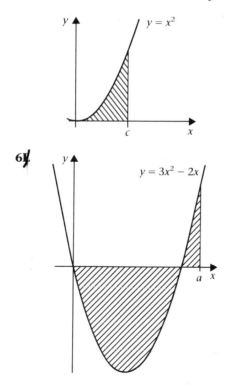

6 Find a such that

$$\int_0^a (3x^2 - 2x) \, dx = 0$$

5.5 The indefinite integral

Since $\dfrac{d(x^2 + 5x)}{dx} = 2x + 5$ you know that

$$\int_1^2 (2x + 5)\, dx = \left[x^2 + 5x \right]_1^2 = 8$$

Differentiate each of

$$x^2 + 5x + 1, \quad x^2 + 5x + 4, \quad x^2 + 5x - 3.$$

Explain why each of these functions could be used as an integral function for $2x + 5$ and why each gives the same answer for

$$\int_1^2 (2x + 5)\, dx$$

To evaluate an integral such as $\displaystyle\int_3^5 (2x)\, dx$ you can use **any** integral function of the form $x^2 + c$ where c is a constant, known as the **constant of integration**. Some examples of constants of integration in various contexts are given on tasksheet 5.

TASKSHEET 5 — Constants of integration (page 93)

A general integral function such as $x^2 + c$ is called an **indefinite integral**.

An integral sign without any limits is used to denote indefinite integrals. A constant term '+c' should always be included, for example:

$$\int (2x)\, dx = x^2 + c$$

$$\int x^2\, dx = \tfrac{1}{3} x^3 + c$$

Integrals between limits, for example:

$$\int_3^5 (2x)\, dx = 16$$

are called **definite integrals**. A definite integral has a (definite) numerical value.

For definite integrals, there is no need to include the constant of integration because it cancels out as shown in the following example:

$$\int_1^3 x^2 \, dx = \left[\tfrac{1}{3}x^3 + c \right]_1^3$$

$$= (9 + c) - (\tfrac{1}{3} + c)$$

$$= 8\tfrac{2}{3} \quad \text{(irrespective of the value of } c.\text{)}$$

You can therefore simply write

$$\int_1^3 x^2 \, dx = \left[\tfrac{1}{3}x^3 \right]_1^3$$

$$= 9 - \tfrac{1}{3}$$

$$= 8\tfrac{2}{3}$$

EXAMPLE 5

Find y as a function of x given that $y = 10$ when $x = 1$ and that

$$\frac{dy}{dx} = (3x - 1)(x + 3)$$

SOLUTION

$$y = \int (3x - 1)(x + 3) \, dx$$

$$= \int (3x^2 + 8x - 3) \, dx$$

$$= x^3 + 4x^2 - 3x + c$$

But $y = 10$ when $x = 1$

$$\Rightarrow 10 = 1 + 4 - 3 + c$$
$$\Rightarrow c = 8$$
$$\Rightarrow y = x^3 + 4x^2 - 3x + 8$$

EXERCISE 4

1 Find the following:

(a) $\int (x^3 - 1) \, dx$ (b) $\int_1^3 (x + 1)(x - 2) \, dx$

2   Find y as a function of x, if

(a) $\dfrac{dy}{dx} = x - 4$ (b) $\dfrac{dy}{dx} = 3x^2 + x$

(c) $\dfrac{dy}{dx} = x^2 + x + 1$ (d) $\dfrac{dy}{dx} = (x + 1)(x - 2)$

3   Express y as a function of x if:

(a) $\dfrac{dy}{dx} = 3x^2 + 4x$ and the (x, y) graph passes through $(1, 5)$.

(b) $\dfrac{dy}{dx} = x^2 + x + 1$ and the (x, y) graph passes through $(0, 3)$.

4   (a) If $\displaystyle\int_a^b (3x^2 - 2x + 5)\, dx = \left[\, f(x) \,\right]_a^b$, write down a possible $f(x)$.

(b) If $\displaystyle\int_c^d (2t + 1)(t - 4)\, dt = \left[\, k(t) \,\right]_c^d$, find a suitable $k(t)$.

Good
(see p65)

After working through this chapter you should:

1   understand what is meant by a definite integral;

2   understand what is meant by an indefinite integral and the need for a constant of integration;

3   be able to integrate polynomial functions and know that

$$\int (af(x) + bg(x))\, dx = a\int f(x)\,dx + b\int g(x)\, dx$$

4   be able to find areas by using combinations of appropriate integrals;

5   be able to integrate algebraically by using the fact that integration is the inverse process of differentiation:

$$\int_a^b f'(x)\, dx = f(b) - f(a)$$

REVIEW SHEET E

Finding integral functions

$A(u) = \displaystyle\int_0^u x^2 \, dx$ is the area shaded.

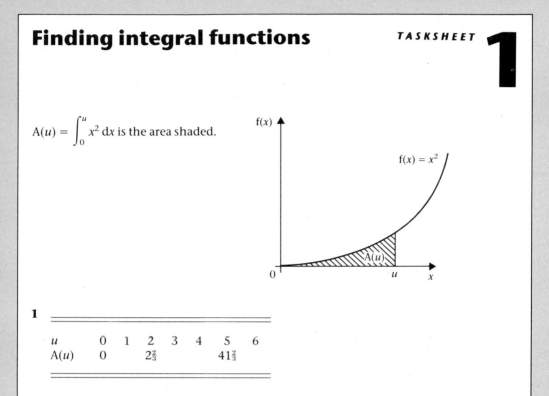

1

u	0	1	2	3	4	5	6
$A(u)$	0		$2\frac{2}{3}$			$41\frac{2}{3}$	

Using the mid-ordinate rule, estimate the values of $A(u)$ missing from the table above.

2 Use the completed table of question 1 to estimate

(a) $\displaystyle\int_2^4 x^2 \, dx$ (b) $\displaystyle\int_1^3 x^2 \, dx$

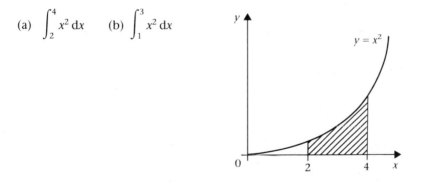

3 (a) Use the completed table from question 1 to draw the graph of $A(u)$ against u.

(b) Use suitable values from your graph to estimate

(i) $\displaystyle\int_{2.5}^{3.1} x^2 \, dx$ (ii) $\displaystyle\int_{0.7}^{3.8} x^2 \, dx$

(c) Suggest a formula for $A(u)$ in terms of u.

Polynomials

1 (a) Sketch the graphs of $y = x^2$ and $y = 2x^2$.

   (b) Shade the areas represented by the integrals

$$\int_0^5 x^2 \, dx \quad \text{and} \quad \int_0^5 2x^2 \, dx$$

   (c) What simple geometrical transformation connects the two areas?

   (d) What will be the connection between $\int_a^b kx^2 \, dx$ and $\int_a^b x^2 \, dx$?

2 (a) Explain, with the aid of a copy of the graph of $y = 2x + 3$, why

$$\int_0^u (2x + 3) \, dx = \left[x^2 + 3x \right]_0^u$$

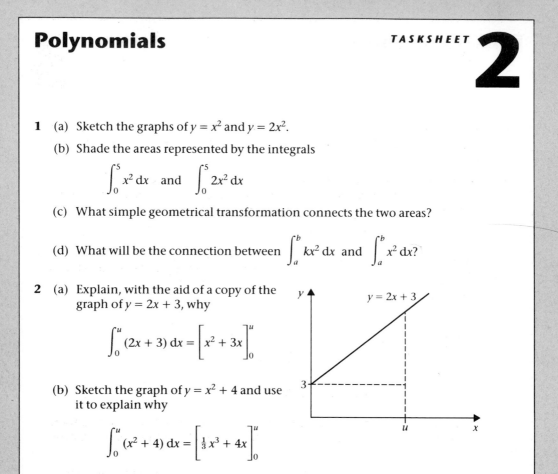

   (b) Sketch the graph of $y = x^2 + 4$ and use it to explain why

$$\int_0^u (x^2 + 4) \, dx = \left[\tfrac{1}{3} x^3 + 4x \right]_0^u$$

You may find it helpful to use a graph plotter with an 'area' option to answer the following questions. Guidance is given on technology datasheet: *Area functions*.

3 Choose two functions of the form $ax^2 + bx + c$, where a, b and c are constants. (Do not always choose positive values for a, b and c.) Write down probable integral functions and check these either with a graph plotter, or by numerical integration with suitable limits.

4 Suggest a general formula for the integral function of any quadratic.

5 Repeat question 3 for a function of the form $ax^3 + bx^2 + cx + d$.

6 Suggest a general formula for the integral function of any cubic.

Catalyst renewal

You may know that a catalyst is often necessary to promote a chemical reaction. As the reaction goes on, the efficiency of the catalyst diminishes, until eventually it has to be renewed.

Suppose a chemical plant can produce a desired chemical at a rate of 100 kg per hour when the catalyst is fresh but that this productivity gradually decreases in such a way that after t hours the productivity has fallen to a value p kg per hour, where

$$p = 4(t - 5)^2$$

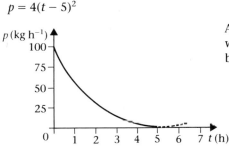

After 5 hours the catalyst has no effect whatsoever, so the graph does not apply beyond this point.

MAXIMISING PRODUCTION

Clearly, what is important is the total amount of chemical produced in a given period of time and not the rate at which it is being produced (the productivity) at any particular time.

Suppose the catalyst is renewed after 3 hours. The production manager would want to know how much chemical is produced in this time. You can see that as one axis of the graph represents time in hours and the other represents productivity in kg hour^{-1}, the area under the graph will represent amount in kilograms.

$$\frac{\text{kg}}{\text{hour}} \times \text{hour} = \text{kg}$$

The total production of chemical is therefore given by the area under the graph.

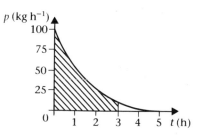

The amount of chemical produced during the first 3 hours is

$$\int_0^3 4(t - 5)^2 \, dt = 4 \int_0^3 (t^2 - 10t + 25) \, dt$$

1 Integrate algebraically to find the amount of chemical produced in the first 3 hours.

TASKSHEET **3**

When the catalyst is renewed the whole plant is shut down. Suppose it takes 30 minutes to change the catalyst. In this case, the plant works on a 3.5-hour production cycle which can be shown graphically

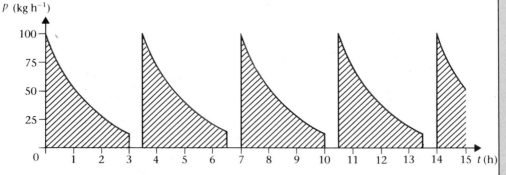

2 (a) What is the average output per hour (average productivity) for a complete production cycle?

 (b) Suppose the catalyst is changed after 1.5 hours (i.e. the plant works on a 2-hour production cycle as it still takes 30 minutes to change the catalyst). Use the integral function you obtained in question 1 to find the average productivity.

 (c) Suppose the catalyst is changed after 40 minutes. What would the average productivity be now?

3 The production manager wants to maximise production (i.e. run the plant so that as much chemical as possible is produced). Investigate different time intervals and determine the frequency with which the catalyst should be changed. Give your answer to the nearest minute.

MAXIMISING PROFIT

Suppose that the chemical is sold at a fixed price of £3 per kg and that there is a cost of £150 each time the catalyst is renewed, with other production costs are more or less fixed at £50 per hour.

The company is not sure that maximising production is necessarily the same as maximising profit.

4E (a) If the catalyst is renewed every 3 hours, what profit does the company make on each kilogram of chemical sold?

 (b) How much profit does the company make per hour in this case?

5E Investigate the profit per kilogram and profit per hour for other time intervals between catalyst renewal. To maximise annual profit, should the company maximise production, profit per kilogram, or profit per hour?

GOOD BUT HARD.

Straight line segments

Go through with them

The gradient of a line segment joining two points is constant. For example:

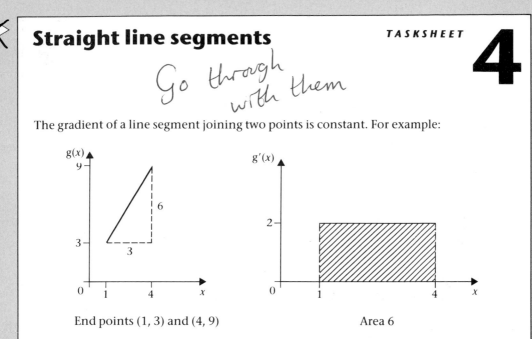

End points (1, 3) and (4, 9)   Area 6

1 Draw diagrams similar to those above for line segments joining the points:

(a) (1, 2), (5, 6)   (b) (4, 8), (6, 2)   (c) (3, 5), (6, 5)

Can you spot a connection between the y-coordinates of the end points of the function and the area under the graph of the derived function?

Explain this connection by considering the definition of the gradient of a straight line.

When the graph of $g(x)$ is a **series** of connected line segments, the diagrams obtained are like those below.

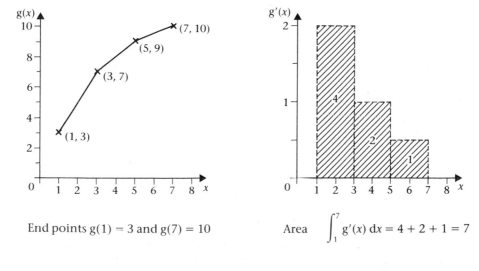

End points $g(1) = 3$ and $g(7) = 10$ Area $\int_{1}^{7} g'(x)\,dx = 4 + 2 + 1 = 7$

2 The following diagrams show two further ways of joining the end points (1, 3) and (7, 10) with three line segments.

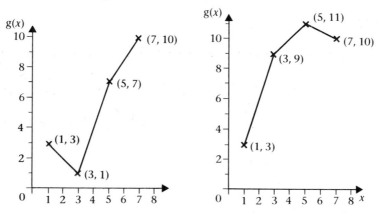

Sketch the graph of the function $g'(x)$ for each of the examples shown above, or any two similar examples of your own invention. In each case,

find $\int_1^7 g'(x)\, dx$. Is it always true that $\int_1^7 g'(x)\, dx = g(7) - g(1)$?

3 Is it always true that $\int_a^b g'(x)\, dx = g(b) - g(a)$? Test this conjecture with **any** similar type of function of your own choice consisting of several line segments.

4E (a) The graph shows a derived function $g'(x)$. Construct a possible graph of the original function $g(x)$.

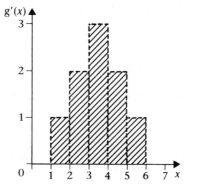

(b) Explain why your answer to (a) is not unique. Construct another possible graph of $g(x)$.

(c) In each case, check that
$$\int_1^6 g'(x)dx = g(6) - g(1).$$

Constants of integration

This tasksheet considers several situations involving constants of integration.

FAMILIES OF CURVES

Any line with gradient 2 has equation of the form $y = 2x + c$, where c is the intercept.

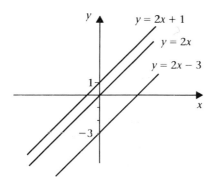

c can be thought of as a constant of integration.

$$\frac{dy}{dx} = 2 \iff y = 2x + c$$

Such a constant of integration can be found if you know any point on the line.

1   Find the equation of the line with gradient 2 passing through (1, 5). At what point does this line cross the y-axis?

2   Sketch a few members of the family of curves which have gradient function

$$\frac{dy}{dx} = 2x$$

Find the equation of the graph which passes through $(2, -1)$ and has $2x$ as its gradient function.

RATES OF CHANGE

In an example from chapter 1, the volume $V\,\text{cm}^3$ of water in a container satisfied

$$\frac{dV}{dt} = -40\,500$$

where t was the time in minutes. The formula for V was therefore of the form

$$V = c - 40\,500t$$

where c was the constant of integration.

3 If the container originally contained 256 500 cm^3 of water, then

(a) find c;

(b) find the time taken for the container to empty.

4 The population of a certain country increases by approximately 0.2 million per year. Find an expression for the population P million in year t, remembering to include the constant of integration.

Given that the population was roughly 38 million in 1900, estimate the population in 2000.

KINEMATICS

If you know the speed $v\,\mathrm{m\,s}^{-1}$ of an object at time t seconds, then a formula for its displacement s metres can be found from

$$\frac{\mathrm{d}s}{\mathrm{d}t} = v$$

For example: suppose that in an experiment a sphere is released from rest on a ramp. Suppose further that its speed t seconds later is given by $4t\,\mathrm{m\,s}^{-1}$

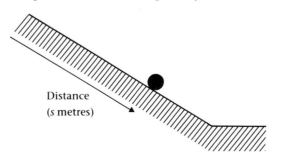

Distance
(s metres)

5 Show that $s = 2t^2 + c$, where c is the constant of integration. What information is provided by the value of c in this case?

6 Write s in terms of t if the sphere is released 0.5 m from the top of the ramp. Find the length of the ramp if the sphere then takes 1 second to reach the bottom.

7 Write s in terms of t if the sphere is released 1 m from the top of the ramp. How long will it then take to reach the bottom of the ramp?

AREAS

The area under a curve does not have to be measured from the $x = 0$ line. For example:

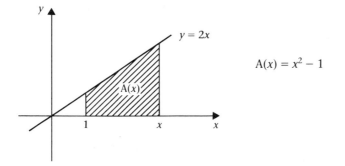

$$A(x) = x^2 - 1$$

8E $x^2 - 9$ is a function for the area under the graph of $y = 2x$. From which line is the area measured?

9E   Suppose that $x^2 - 4x + 4$ is an area function. Deduce the original function and from which value of x the area is measured.

Solutions

1 Rates of change

1.1 Introduction

> What symbol would be used for the gradient of a (time, distance) or (t, s) graph, and what physical quantity would this gradient represent?

$\dfrac{ds}{dt}$ is the symbol used for the gradient of a (t, s) graph. This represents the change in distance per unit of time, which is speed.

E X E R C I S E   1

1 (a) 3 (b) 3

2 (a) Difference in y-coordinates $= -6$, difference in x-coordinates $= 2$

(b) $\dfrac{dy}{dx} = \dfrac{-6}{2} = -3$

3
(a) -7 (b) 1 (c) -2 (d) $\dfrac{1}{2}$

4 (a) Difference in y-coordinates $= -2$, difference in x-coordinates $= 4$

(b) $\dfrac{dy}{dx} = \dfrac{-2}{4} = -\dfrac{1}{2}$

5 (a) $y = \dfrac{1}{2}x + 2 \ \Rightarrow\ \dfrac{dy}{dx} = \dfrac{1}{2}$ (b) $y = -x + 7 \ \Rightarrow\ \dfrac{dy}{dx} = -1$

(c) $-y = -x + 6 \ \Rightarrow\ y = x - 6 \ \Rightarrow\ \dfrac{dy}{dx} = 1$

(d) $2y = -x + 4 \ \Rightarrow\ y = -\dfrac{1}{2}x + 2 \ \Rightarrow\ \dfrac{dy}{dx} = -\dfrac{1}{2}$

6 (a) $C = 702 + 2.87n$ (b) $\dfrac{dC}{dn} = 2.87$. This represents the extra

cost (change in cost) for each unit used.

7 (a) $\dfrac{ds}{dt} = -8$ (b) $\dfrac{dy}{dt} = 4$ (c) $\dfrac{dz}{dy} = -1$ (d) $\dfrac{dy}{dx} = 10$

(e) $y = 12 - 20x \Rightarrow \dfrac{dy}{dx} = -20$

8 (a) $\dfrac{dC}{dr} = 2\pi$. This is by how much the circumference increases when the radius increases by one unit.

(b) Using the result of (a), an extra $2 \times 2\pi = 4\pi$ metres would be needed (neglecting any deviation of the equator from a perfect circle).

(c) Surprisingly, this would still be 4π metres.

1.2 Linear functions

Write down $\dfrac{dh}{dt}$ and $\dfrac{dV}{dt}$ and explain the simple relationship between these rates of change.

$h = 95 - 15t$ ① $V = 2700(95 - 15t)$ ③

$\Rightarrow \dfrac{dh}{dt} = -15$ ② $\Rightarrow V = 2700 \times 95 - 2700 \times 15t$

$\Rightarrow \dfrac{dV}{dt} = -2700 \times 15$ ④

Substituting ① in ②, $V = 2700h$

Substituting ③ in ④, $\dfrac{dV}{dt} = 2700 \dfrac{dh}{dt}$

A generalisation of this idea is that, for any constant a,

$$y = au \Rightarrow \dfrac{dy}{dx} = a \dfrac{du}{dx}$$

E X E R C I S E 2

1 $\dfrac{dy}{dx} = 5$ (gradient)

So the line has equation $y = 5x + c$. $(-1, 2)$ is a point on the line, so

$2 = 5 \times -1 + c \Rightarrow c = 7$

The equation is $y = 5x + 7$.

2 (a) $y = -2x + 8$ (b) $s = \tfrac{1}{2}t + 1$ (c) $p = \tfrac{2}{3}x + 3$

3 $\dfrac{dy}{dx} = \dfrac{6}{3} \Rightarrow \dfrac{dy}{dx} = 2, \quad y = 2x + 3$

4 (a) (i) $C = 5 + 7t$ (ii) $\dfrac{dC}{dt} = 7$

(b) (i) $\dfrac{dC}{dt} = 6$ (ii) $C = 8 + 6t$

5

Test mark, T	25	26	49	50
Rescaled mark, R	0	4	96	100

(a) $\dfrac{dR}{dT} = 4$ (b) $R = 4T - 100$

6 (a) $P = 38 + \frac{10}{50}t$ or $P = 38 + 0.2t$

(b) $\dfrac{dP}{dt} = 0.2$. The population is increasing by 0.2 million each year.

(c) For 1990, $P = 38 + 0.2 \times 90 = 56$ millions

This may be reasonably close to the actual population. However, 1990 is outside the first half of the century so the simple linear model is being applied inappropriately. During the second half of the twentieth century the population growth has been more irregular.

7 (a) $\dfrac{du}{dx} = 2, \quad \dfrac{dy}{dx} = -4$

(b) (i) $2 + (-4) = -2$ (ii) $2 - (-4) = 6$ (iii) $3 \times 2 + (-4) = 2$

(iv) $2 - 3 \times (-4) = 14$ (v) $3 \times 2 + 2 \times (-4) = -2$

(vi) $2 \times 2 - 3 \times (-4) = 16$

(c) (i) $y = (4 + 2x) + (5 - 4x)$, so $y = 9 - 2x$

(ii) $y = -1 + 6x$ (iii) $y = 17 + 2x$ (iv) $y = -11 + 14x$

(v) $y = 22 - 2x$ (vi) $y = -7 + 16x$

8   (a) $s = 15 + \dfrac{f - 200}{15}, \qquad \dfrac{\mathrm{d}s}{\mathrm{d}f} = \dfrac{1}{15}$

The change in steaming time is $\frac{1}{15}$ minutes (4 seconds) for each extra gram of flour.

(b) $p = 25 + \dfrac{f - 200}{15}, \qquad \dfrac{\mathrm{d}p}{\mathrm{d}f} = \dfrac{1}{15}$

The change in pressure time is $\frac{1}{15}$ minutes (4 seconds) for each extra gram of flour.

(c) $T = s + p \;\Rightarrow\; \dfrac{\mathrm{d}T}{\mathrm{d}f} = \dfrac{\mathrm{d}s}{\mathrm{d}f} + \dfrac{\mathrm{d}p}{\mathrm{d}f}$

$$\dfrac{\mathrm{d}T}{\mathrm{d}f} = \dfrac{2}{15}$$

The change in total cooking time is $\frac{2}{15}$ minutes (8 seconds) for each extra gram of flour.

2   Gradients of curves

2.1   Locally straight curves

> Use the picture to estimate the gradient of the hill at this point.

Notice that the snow surface appears to be flat or straight close to the skier.

The gradient is approximately 0.5.

Note that the mathematical definition of gradient ignores the direction in which the skier is pointing.

> When you zoom in, how is the local straight line that you see related to the tangent line?

When you zoom into a curve at a point, the local straight line is part of the tangent to the curve at that point. Consequently, the gradient of the curve and the gradient of the tangent to the curve are equal at this point.

2.5 Finding gradients numerically

> (a) How close should (u, v) be to $(3, 9)$?
>
> (b) Suggest coordinates for (u, v).

(a) The closer you take (u, v) to $(3, 9)$, the better will be the approximation to the gradient of the curve at $(3, 9)$; so the closer the better, within the limitations of your calculator.

(b) Possible values are $(3.1, 3.1^2)$, $(3.01, 3.01^2)$, $(3.001, 3.001^2)$ and so on. These give values for the gradient of 6.1, 6.01, 6.001 etc.

2.6 Gradient functions

EXERCISE 1

1 (a) $\dfrac{dy}{dx} = 6x$ (b) $\dfrac{dv}{du} = 15u^2 - 4u$

  (c) $\dfrac{dy}{dx} = -2x$ (d) $\dfrac{ds}{dt} = 4 - 2t$

2 (a) $\dfrac{dy}{dx} = 10x$ (b) (i) 10   (ii) 20   (iii) -10

3 (a) $\dfrac{dy}{dx} = -6x^2$

  When $x = 0$, gradient = 0.
  When $x = 2$, gradient = -24.

  (b) $\dfrac{dy}{dx} = 5 - 2x$

  When $x = 2$, gradient = 1.
  When $x = 4$, gradient = -3.

4 (a) $\dfrac{dy}{dx} = 2 - 2x$.   At $(2, 3)$, $\dfrac{dy}{dx} = 2 - 2 \times 2 = -2$.

  The tangent passes through $(2, 3)$ and has gradient -2. Its equation is therefore $y - 3 = -2 (x - 2)$, or $y = -2x + 7$.

  (b) $\dfrac{dy}{dx} = 3x^2$.   At $(2, 3)$, $\dfrac{dy}{dx} = 12$.

  The equation of the tangent is $y = 12x - 21$.

(c) $\dfrac{dy}{dx} = 2x - 3x^2$.   At $(2, 3)$, $\dfrac{dy}{dx} = -8$.

The equation of the tangent is $y = -8x + 19$.

5 $\dfrac{dy}{dx} = 1 + 4x$.

When $x = 3$, $\dfrac{dy}{dx} = 13$ and $y = 21$.

The equation of the tangent is $y - 21 = 13(x - 3)$, or $y = 13x - 18$.

6   (a) $\dfrac{dy}{dx} = 1 - 3x^2$.   At $(0, 5)$, the gradient is 1.

The equation of the tangent is $y - 5 = x - 0$, or $y = x + 5$.

(b) $\dfrac{dy}{dx} = -3 + 6x^2$.   At $(0, 5)$, the gradient is -3.

The equation of the tangent is $y - 5 = -3(x - 0)$, or $y = 5 - 3x$.

(c) $\dfrac{dy}{dx} = 8x + 9x^2$.   At $(0, 5)$, the gradient is 0.

The tangent is therefore horizontal and as it passes through $(0, 5)$ its equation is $y = 5$.

3 Optimisation

3.1 Graphs and gradient graphs

In (a), how do you know that the quadratic curve is not the other way up?

Carefully justify the alternative solution to (c):

$$x = \frac{0+5}{2} = 2.5$$

The coefficient of x^2 in $x^2 - 5x$ is $+1$ and so the quadratic is $\bigcup$-shaped.

Quadratics are symmetrical about their axes and so the x-coordinate of the two points where the x-axis is crossed can be averaged to find the x-coordinate of the vertex.

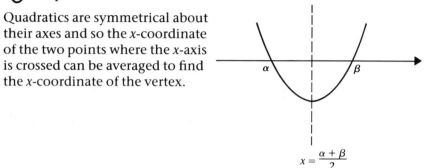

$$x = \frac{\alpha + \beta}{2}$$

E X E R C I S E   1

1 $y = (x - 1)(x - 2)(x - 4)$

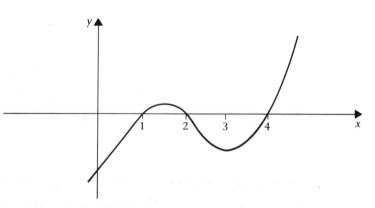

The coordinates of the stationary points could be determined precisely by using calculus. (Note that the stationary points are **not** at $x = 1.5$ and $x = 3$.)

2 (a)

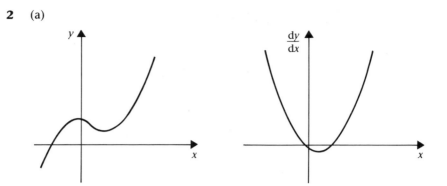

Zeros of the gradient graph correspond to stationary points on the (x, y) graph. The sign of $\dfrac{dy}{dx}$ corresponds to the sign of the gradient on the (x, y) graph.

(b)

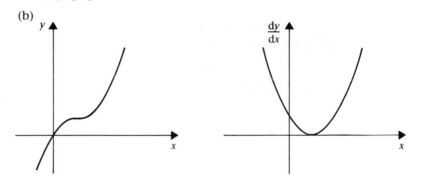

The stationary point on the (x, y) graph corresponds to the single zero on the gradient graph. $\dfrac{dy}{dx}$ is positive for all other values of x because the gradient of the (x, y) graph is positive everywhere except at the stationary point.

(c)

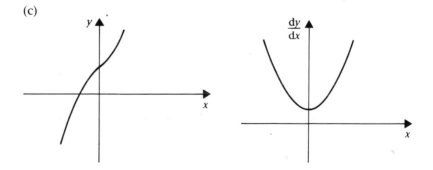

The gradient graph has no zeros because there are no stationary points on the (x, y) graph. $\dfrac{dy}{dx}$ is always positive, and so is the gradient of the (x, y) graph.

3

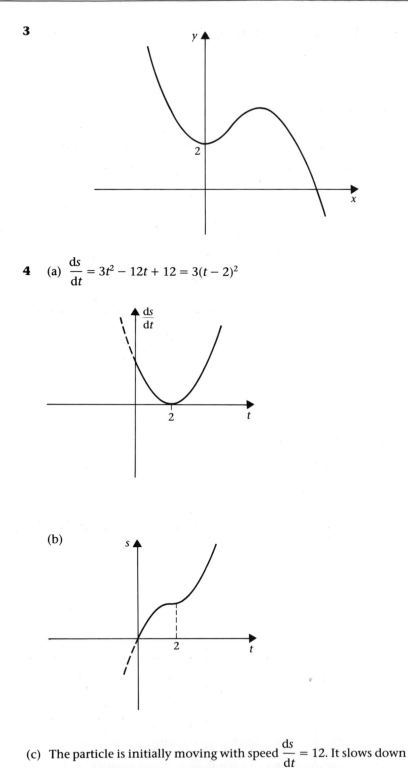

4 (a) $\dfrac{ds}{dt} = 3t^2 - 12t + 12 = 3(t-2)^2$

(b)

(c) The particle is initially moving with speed $\dfrac{ds}{dt} = 12$. It slows down until it comes to rest instantaneously when $t = 2$. It then speeds up again and increases in speed forever.

3.2   Quadratics and cubics

E X E R C I S E   2

1 $\dfrac{dy}{dx} = 3x^2 - 12 = 3(x^2 - 4)$

The stationary points occur when $\dfrac{dy}{dx} = 0$, that is when $x = 2$ or -2. The stationary points are $(2, -11)$ and $(-2, 21)$.

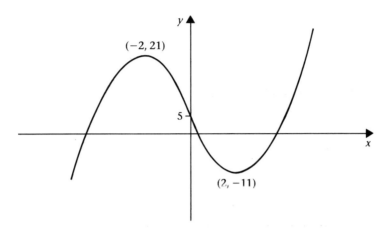

2 $\dfrac{dy}{dx} = 6x^2 - 18x + 12$

$\qquad = 6(x^2 - 3x + 2)$

$\qquad = 6(x - 1)(x - 2)$

$\dfrac{dy}{dx} = 0$ when $x = 1$ or $x = 2$. The stationary points are $(1, -2)$ and $(2, -3)$.

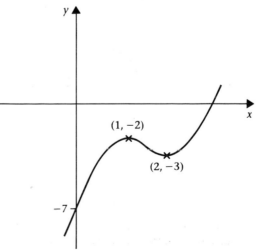

3 (a) (i) $y = 5x - x^2 = x(5 - x)$

$\dfrac{dy}{dx} = 0$ for $x = 2.5$

(ii) maximum at $(2.5, 6.25)$

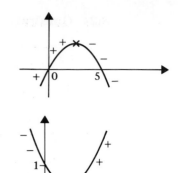

(b) (i) $y = (1 - x)^2 = 1 - 2x + x^2$

$\dfrac{dy}{dx} = 0$ for $x = 1$

(ii) minimum at $(1, 0)$

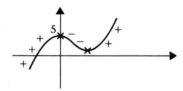

(c) (i) $y = x^3 - 3x^2 + 5$

$\dfrac{dy}{dx} = 0$ for $x = 0$, $x = 2$

(ii) maximum at $(0, 5)$, minimum at $(2, 1)$

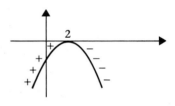

(d) (i) $y = 4x - x^2 - 4$

$\dfrac{dy}{dx} = 0$ for $x = 2$

(ii) maximum at $(2, 0)$

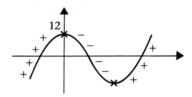

(e) (i) $y = 2x^3 - 9x^2 + 12$

$\dfrac{dy}{dx} = 0$ for $x = 0$, $x = 3$

(ii) maximum at $(0, 12)$, minimum at $(3, -15)$

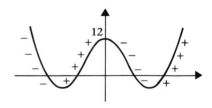

(f) (i) $y = x^4 - 8x^2 + 12$

$\dfrac{dy}{dx} = 0$ for $x = 0$, $x = \pm 2$

(ii) maximum at $(0, 12)$, minima at $(2, -4)$ and $(-2, -4)$

4 (a) $+6, +3, 0$. The quadratic has reflection symmetry and so

B's x-coordinate is $\dfrac{+6+0}{2}$.

(b) $+6, +4, 0$. The cubic does **not** have reflection symmetry.

3.3   Maxima and minima

> Without doing any calculations, write down what you think happens to the volume of the cylinder as it changes from a tall thin cylinder to a short fat cylinder as shown below.
>
> Draw a rough sketch of a graph which shows these changes in volume.

Volume increases, reaches a maximum, then decreases. In terms of the radius of the cylinder, you might expect the volume to vary as shown in this graph.

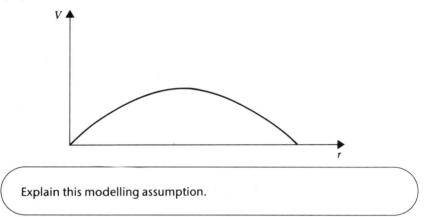

> Explain this modelling assumption.

On the (I, N) graph you know the two marked points.

If you assume a linear relationship between N and I you obtain the straight line shown. This has equation

$N = 20 - \frac{1}{2}I$

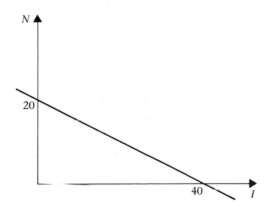

E X E R C I S E   3

1 $f = 25 + v - 0.012v^2, \quad 30 \leq v \leq 80$
(The inequality for v suggests that the car is in top gear.)

(a) $\dfrac{df}{dv} = 1 - 0.024v$

v	35	60
f	45.3	41.8
$\dfrac{df}{dv}$	0.16	−0.44

At the higher speed, the number of miles per gallon is lower.
At 35 m.p.h., the number of miles per gallon **increases** with increasing speed. At 60 m.p.h. it **decreases**.

(b) $\dfrac{df}{dv} = 0$ when $v = 41.7$. The most economical speed is 41.7 m.p.h.

2 $n = 30 - 2P, \quad R = 30P - 2P^2$

(a) $\dfrac{dR}{dP} = 30 - 4P$ gives the rate at which revenue from the items changes with their price.

(b)   When $P = 5$, $\dfrac{dR}{dP} = 10$.   When $P = 10$, $\dfrac{dR}{dP} = -10$.

(c) $\dfrac{dR}{dP} = 30 - 4P$ must be positive and so $P < 7.50$.

(d)   £7.50. At this price, $\dfrac{dR}{dP} = 0$.

3   One of several ways of labelling the quantities involved is to let h be the variable height of the gutter.

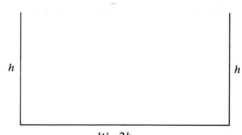

h h

$W - 2h$

The cross-sectional area A is then given by

$$A = (20 - 2h)h = 20 - 2h^2$$

$$\frac{dA}{dh} = 20 - 4h$$

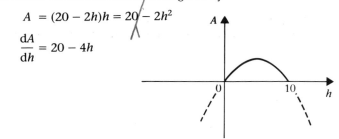

The area is maximised when $h = 5$.

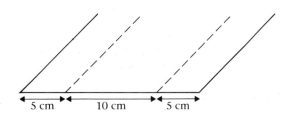

5 cm   10 cm   5 cm

4   (a) $P = 500 + 100t$

$$\frac{dP}{dt} = 100$$

This represents the rate at which the population is increasing each year.

(b) $P = 100(5 + t - 0.25t^2)$

$$\frac{dP}{dt} = 100 - 50t$$

$$t = 1, \frac{dP}{dt} = 50; \quad t = 2, \frac{dP}{dt} = 0; \quad t = 3, \frac{dP}{dt} = -50$$

The population stopped increasing after 2 years, and then it decreased. The maximum population occurred when $t = 2$ and was

$$100(5 + 2 - 0.25 \times 2^2) = 600$$

The population decreased to zero and so the estate was abandoned.

4 Numerical integration

4.1 Areas under graphs

E X E R C I S E 1

1 (a) km (b) miles (c) cm^3 (d) g

2 $\frac{1}{60}$th of a revolution

4.2 Estimating areas

> You could have estimated the amount of fuel used more accurately by using the trapezium rule with eight strips. Would this have over- or under-estimated the actual area?

Because the gradient of the curve is increasing, the trapezium rule will always over-estimate the area.

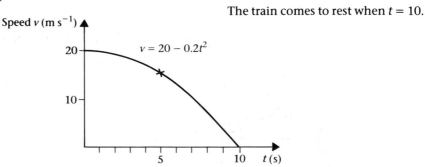

E X E R C I S E 2

1

Speed v (m s^{-1})

The train comes to rest when $t = 10$.

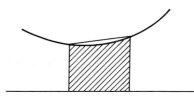

$$v = 20 - 0.2t^2$$

By the trapezium rule, the area under the graph from $t = 0$ to $t = 10$ is approximately

$$\tfrac{1}{2} \times 2 \times (20 + 19.2) + \tfrac{1}{2} \times 2 \times (19.2 + 16.8) + \tfrac{1}{2} \times 2 \times (16.8 + 12.8)$$
$$+ \tfrac{1}{2} \times 2 \,(12.8 + 7.2) + \tfrac{1}{2} \times 2 \times (7.2 + 0) = 132$$

The distance travelled is about 132 m.

2 (a) Assuming that the cross-section is always circular, you can first calculate the cross-sectional area, A, from the circumference, C, by the formula

$$A = \frac{C^2}{4\pi}$$

Height, h (cm)	10	30	50	70	90
Area, A (cm^2)	198.9	127.3	71.6	31.8	8.0

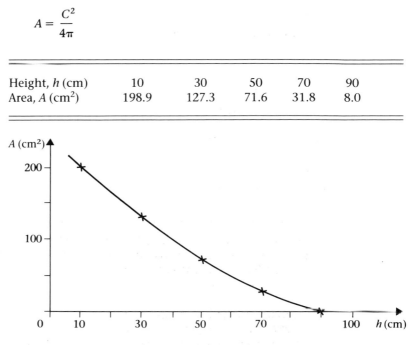

(b) Area under graph $\approx 20[198.9 + 127.3 + 71.6 + 31.8 + 8.0]$
≈ 8750

This area represents the volume of the stalagmite in cm^3.

4.3 Integration

EXERCISE 3

1

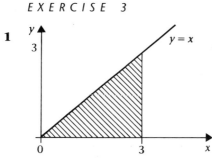

The integral represents the area under the graph of $y = x$ between $x = 0$ and $x = 3$.

This is the area of a triangle (shaded), $\frac{1}{2} \times 3 \times 3 = 4.5$. Thus $\displaystyle\int_0^3 x \, dx = 4.5$.

2 (a) (area of trapezium) $\quad 3 \times \frac{5}{2} = 7.5$

(b) (area of rectangle) $\quad 10$

(c) (area of trapezium) $\quad 3 \times \frac{1}{2}(5 + 11) = 24$

3 (a) $10t \, \text{m s}^{-1}$ (assuming it is dropped from rest)

(b) $\int_0^5 10t \, \mathrm{d}t$

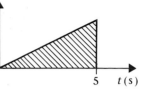

(c) Area of triangle shaded, $\frac{5}{2} \times 50 = 125\,\text{m}$

4 $\sqrt{(10 - 1.5^2)} + \sqrt{(10 - 2.5^2)} = 4.72$

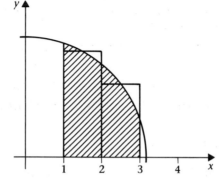

4.4 Numerical methods

Explain why the area of trapezium B is precisely the same as the area of rectangle A.

Area B is equal to area A because the two shaded areas are equal.

E X E R C I S E 4

1 (a) Too small (b) Neither – exactly the same (c) Not clearly too large or too small (d) Too large

2 (a) Too large (b) Exact (c) Not clear (d) Too small

3 Type A: Shaded area $\approx 6\frac{2}{3}\,\text{cm}^2$
Volume $\quad \approx 6\frac{2}{3} \times 80 \approx 533\,\text{cm}^3$

Type B: Shaded area $\approx 4\frac{2}{3}\,\text{cm}^2$
Volume $\quad \approx 4\frac{2}{3} \times 15 \approx 70\,\text{cm}^3$

Total needed $\approx (533 \times 12\,000) + (70 \times 8000)\,\text{cm}^3$
$\approx 6.96 \times 10^6\,\text{cm}^3$
$\approx 6.96\,\text{m}^3$

Adding 5% gives $6.96 \times 1.05 \approx 7.3\,\text{m}^3$.

4.5 'Negative' areas

State what **area** represents in the graph above and explain the significant difference between 'positive' and 'negative' area in this situation.

From $t = 0$ to $t = 9$, the graph is above the time axis and so the amount of carbon dioxide in the water is increasing. The area represents the total increase in mg per litre.

From $t = 9$ to $t = 17$, the amount is decreasing, the area being under the time axis.

From $t = 17$ to $t = 24$, the area is positive again.

The total area should be zero if it is a **balanced** aquarium.

EXERCISE 5

1 (a) From 5 p.m. until 9 a.m. The increase is about 70 mg.

  (b) The 'negative' area between $t = 9$ and $t = 17$ is also about 70. So the amount dissolved stays roughly constant.

2 (a)
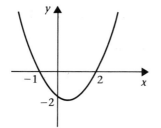
$$y = x^2 - x - 2 = (x + 1)(x - 2)$$

  (b) (i) $26\frac{2}{3}$ (ii) $22\frac{1}{2}$ (iii) $-4\frac{1}{2}$ (iv) $8\frac{2}{3}$

  (c) $4\frac{1}{2}$

3 (a) At $t = 2$ the net flow into the tank is zero. So this is the moment when the water level is highest (it stops rising and begins to fall).

  (b) Area represents change in volume of water in the tank during the appropriate time interval. 'Positive' area represents increase in volume and 'negative' area represents decrease in volume.

  (c) (i) About 10.6. This represents a net increase of 10.6 litres during the first 2 minutes.

    (ii) About -5.0. This represents a net decrease from $t = 2$ to $t = 5$.

    (iii) About 5.6. This represents a net increase from $t = 0$ to $t = 5$.

  (d) 60.6, 55.6 litres. About 24.5 minutes.

5 Algebraic integration

5.1 The integral function

Using this new notation, evaluate $\int_2^5 x^2 \, dx$.

On a sketch of $y = x^2$, shade the area you have found.

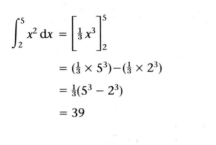

$$\int_2^5 x^2 \, dx = \left[\tfrac{1}{3} x^3 \right]_2^5$$

$$= (\tfrac{1}{3} \times 5^3) - (\tfrac{1}{3} \times 2^3)$$

$$= \tfrac{1}{3}(5^3 - 2^3)$$

$$= 39$$

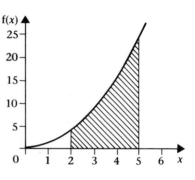

EXERCISE 1

1 (a)

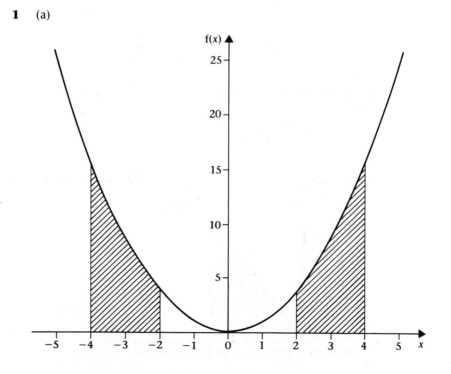

(b) $\displaystyle\int_2^4 x^2\,dx$ and $\displaystyle\int_{-4}^{-2} x^2\,dx$ are the areas of the regions shaded above. By symmetry these are equal.

(c) $\displaystyle\int_2^4 x^2\,dx = \left[\tfrac{1}{3}x^3\right]_2^4 = 18\tfrac{2}{3}.$ Similarly, $\displaystyle\int_{-4}^{-2} x^2\,dx = 18\tfrac{2}{3}.$

2 (a) (i) $\displaystyle\int_{-3}^{-1.5} x^2\,dx = \left[\tfrac{1}{3}x^3\right]_{-3}^{-1.5} = 7.875$

(ii) $\displaystyle\int_{-1.5}^{1.5} x^2\,dx = \left[\tfrac{1}{3}x^3\right]_{-1.5}^{1.5} = 2.250$

(iii) $\displaystyle\int_{1.5}^{3} x^2\,dx = \left[\tfrac{1}{3}x^3\right]_{1.5}^{3} = 7.875$

(iv) $\displaystyle\int_{-1.5}^{3} x^2\,dx = \left[\tfrac{1}{3}x^3\right]_{-1.5}^{3} = 10.125$

(b) $\displaystyle\int_{-3}^{-1.5} x^2\,dx = \int_{1.5}^{3} x^2\,dx$

$\displaystyle\int_{-1.5}^{1.5} x^2\,dx + \int_{1.5}^{3} x^2\,dx = \int_{-1.5}^{3} x^2\,dx$

3 (a) Shaded area $= \tfrac{1}{2} \times u \times 2u = u^2$

(b) $\displaystyle\int_0^u 2x\,dx = \left[x^2\right]_0^u = u^2$

4 (a)
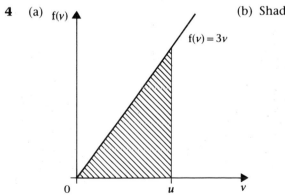
(b) Shaded area $= \tfrac{1}{2} \times u \times 3u = \tfrac{3}{2}u^2$

5 (a) f(x)

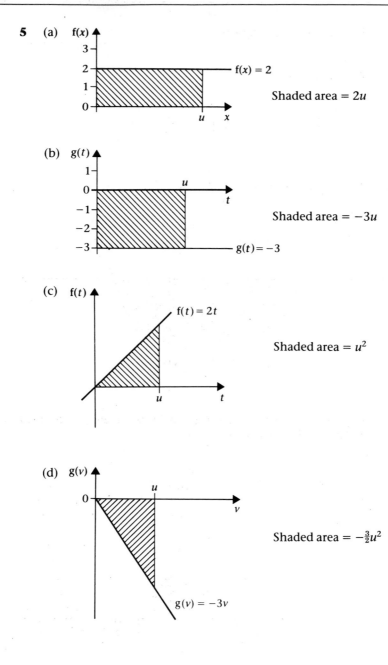

f(x) = 2

Shaded area = 2u

(b) g(t)

Shaded area = −3u

g(t) = −3

(c) f(t)

f(t) = 2t

Shaded area = u²

(d) g(v)

Shaded area = −\frac{3}{2}u²

g(v) = −3v

6 (a) $A(x) = mx$ (b) $A(x) = \frac{1}{2}mx^2$

5.2   Polynomial integrals

Notation P74

E X E R C I S E   2

1   (a) $\displaystyle\int_{2}^{4} (3x^2 - 5)\, dx$ (b) $\left[x^3 - 5x \right]_{2}^{4} = 46$

2   (a) $\displaystyle\int_{-2}^{1} (t^3 + 2t^2 - 3)\, dt = \left[\tfrac{1}{4}t^4 + \tfrac{2}{3}t^3 - 3t \right]_{-2}^{1} = -6\tfrac{3}{4}$

   (b)

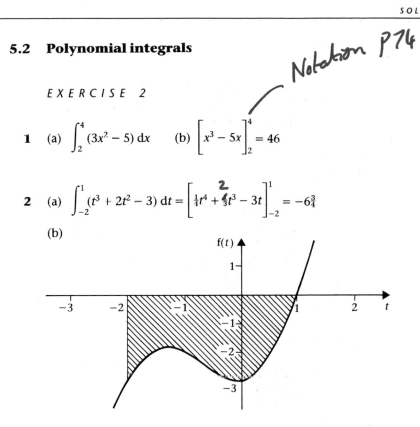

Between $t = -2$ and $t = 1$, the graph lies completely below the t-axis and hence the shaded area is negative.

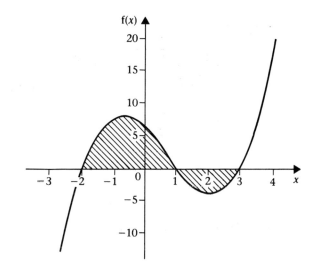

117

(b) $\displaystyle\int_{-2}^{1} (x^3 - 2x^2 - 5x + 6)\,dx = \frac{63}{4}$

$\displaystyle\int_{1}^{3} (x^3 - 2x^2 - 5x + 6)\,dx = -\frac{16}{3}$

The total area is $\frac{63}{4} + \frac{16}{3} = \frac{253}{12} \approx 21.08$.

4 (a) $\displaystyle\int_{0}^{2} 5(5 - 2t)\,dt = 5\int_{0}^{2} (5 - 2t)\,dt$

$$= 5\left[5t - t^2\right]_{0}^{2}$$

$$= 30$$

It travels 30 metres.

(b) It reaches maximum height when $v = 0$. This occurs when $t = 2.5$ seconds.

(c) $\displaystyle\int_{0}^{2.5} 5(5 - 2t)\,dt = 31.25$ (metres)

5.4 The fundamental theorem of calculus

EXERCISE 3

1 (a) (i) 4 (ii) 0

(b)

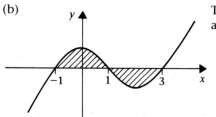

The graph has rotational symmetry about $(1, 0)$.

2 (a) $3x^2 - 10x$

(b) $\left[x^3 - 5x^2 + 7\right]_{1}^{2} = -8$

3 (a) $10x + 3$ (b) $6t^2$

Note that $h(t) = 6t^2$ for **any** integral function of the type $2t^3 + c$ where c is constant.

4 (a) (i) The graphs intersect where $x^2 = 8 - x^2 \Rightarrow x = 2$ (since $x > 0$).
The graph of $y = 8 - x^2$ intersects the x-axis
where $x^2 = 8 \Rightarrow x = \sqrt{8}$.

The integrals arise from
splitting the area as shown.

(ii) $A = \left[\frac{1}{3}x^3\right]_0^2 + \left[8x - \frac{1}{3}x^3\right]_2^{\sqrt{8}} \approx 4.42$

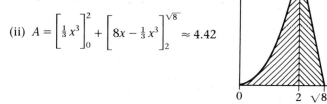

(b) (i) The graphs intersect at $(0, 0)$ and $(1, 1)$. The shaded area is

$$\frac{1}{2} \times 1 \times 1 - \int_0^1 x^2 \, dx$$

$$= \frac{1}{2} - \frac{1}{3} = \frac{1}{6}$$

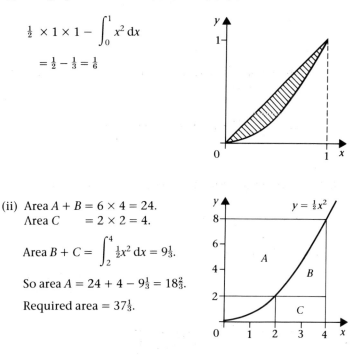

(ii) Area $A + B = 6 \times 4 = 24$.
Area $C \quad = 2 \times 2 = 4$.

Area $B + C = \int_2^4 \frac{1}{2}x^2 \, dx = 9\frac{1}{3}$.

So area $A = 24 + 4 - 9\frac{1}{3} = 18\frac{2}{3}$.

Required area $= 37\frac{1}{3}$.

(iii) The graphs $y = 3x^2 - 12$ and $y = 12 - 3x^2$ both intersect the x-axis
at $x = \pm 2$.

By symmetry, the shaded area is twice the area enclosed by the
curve $y = 12 - 3x^2$ and the x-axis from $x = -2$ to $x = 2$.

$$\text{Shaded area} = 2\int_{-2}^{2} (12 - 3x^2) \, dx = 2\left[12x - x^3\right]_{-2}^{2} = 64$$

119

5 Shaded area $= \displaystyle\int_0^c x^2\,\mathrm{d}x = \left[\tfrac{1}{3}x^3\right]_0^c = \tfrac{1}{3}c^3 = 6$

$\Rightarrow\ c^3 = 18$

$\Rightarrow\ c = \sqrt[3]{18} \approx 2.62.$

6E $\left[x^3 - x^2\right]_0^a = 0$

$\Rightarrow\ a^3 - a^2 = 0$

$\Rightarrow\ a = 0$ (which does not apply here) or $a = 1$

5.5 The indefinite integral

EXERCISE 4

1 (a) $\tfrac{1}{4}x^4 - x + c$

(b) $\displaystyle\int_1^3 (x+1)(x-2)\,\mathrm{d}x = \int_1^3 (x^2 - x - 2)\,\mathrm{d}x$

$$= \left[\tfrac{1}{3}x^3 - \tfrac{1}{2}x^2 - 2x\right]_1^3 = \tfrac{2}{3}$$

2 (a) $y = \tfrac{1}{2}x^2 - 4x + c$

(b) $y = x^3 + \tfrac{1}{2}x^2 + c$

(c) $y = \tfrac{1}{3}x^3 + \tfrac{1}{2}x^2 + x + c$

(d) $(x+1)(x-2) = x^2 - x - 2\ \Rightarrow\ y = \tfrac{1}{3}x^3 - \tfrac{1}{2}x^2 - 2x + c$

3 (a) $y = x^3 + 2x^2 + 2$

(b) $y = \tfrac{1}{3}x^3 + \tfrac{1}{2}x^2 + x + 3$

4 (a) $x^3 - x^2 + 5x$

(b) $(2t+1)(t-4) = 2t^2 - 7t - 4$

$k(t) = \tfrac{2}{3}t^3 - \tfrac{7}{2}t^2 - 4t$